PIANIST'S PROGRESS

PIANIST'S PROGRESS

by
Helen Drees Ruttencutter

Thomas Y. Crowell, Publishers   Established 1834 New York

Much of this work appeared originally in *The New Yorker.*

FIRST EDITION

Designed by Ginger Legato

Library of Congress Cataloging in Publication Data

Ruttencutter, Helen Drees.
    Pianist's progress.

    1. McCabe, Robin. 2. Pianists—United States—
Biography. I. Title.
ML417.M17R9   786.1'092'4 [B]   78-22464
ISBN 0-690-01761-8

79 80 81 82 83 10 9 8 7 6 5 4 3 2 1

For Jim

PIANIST'S PROGRESS

I

Every year, in March and June, the Juilliard School, in New York City, holds auditions for hundreds of musicians from all over the world who hope to be admitted as students the following fall. There is a third audition, in September, for any departments that still have openings. Juilliard is one of a large number of schools throughout the world whose purpose is to turn out performers, and the seriousness of its intentions is made clear in a paragraph of its catalogue under the heading "General Admission Requirements":

> It is assumed that any student accepted for study at Juilliard has made a total commitment to his chosen field and that, in many instances, genuine hardships and sacrifices have been made in order to begin or continue study at the School. This commitment signifies complete dedication to study, work, and performance to the best of the student's capabilities. It also demands no compromise that would affect the standard of excellence expected of the School, its faculty, and its students.

The field of music is an extremely crowded one these days. The explosion, epidemic, pandemic of performers is attributed to a variety of causes: teaching of a higher quality than was common in previous years; the easy availability to everyone of note-perfect recordings by the world's greatest artists (note-perfect because of sophisticated recording equipment that enables record producers, in conjunction with the artists, to splice together the best parts of several recording sessions, even to the point of substituting one note for another); the postwar population growth, which has resulted in more entrants into every field; a hard-to-explain general superiority of the young these days, which shows itself in, among other things, new Olympic records in almost every event and a recent tendency of young musicians to bypass a few years of service in minor symphonies and go straight into major ones, such as the Chicago, the Boston, and the New York.

Among performers, pianists have problems that are unique. The instrument they perform on in public is never their own—with the exception of Vladimir Horowitz, Arthur Rubinstein, and one or two others, who take their pianos with them wherever they play—and, for a number of reasons, it is seldom one they enjoy performing on. One reason is that pianos are not often in perfect tune. Another reason is that their action varies—it may be stiff or loose or somewhere in between. Stiff action can be tiring, but at least the performer knows what he's coping with. Loose action forces him to alter his finger technique—to decrease the speed of finger approach to the keys; keys, when they are struck, normally move slightly sideways, but with very loose action the movement becomes excessive, the result being an eerie slippery feeling. Piano keys are not always of standard measurement. Some years ago, a major piano company experimented with narrower, rounded black keys, and many pianos with these keys are still in use. The difference is enough to cause a pianist's fingers to slip off the keys or, in rapid passages, to miss them entirely. Also, black keys are glued to the surface of the keyboard, and on occasion one can come unglued and go flying into an astonished audience. Furthermore, the white keys are now made of plastic instead of ivory, which causes a pianist's hands to perspire during a performance, increasing the hazard of note-splitting—hitting two keys instead of one. The pedals can be sluggish, squeaky, or even nonfunctioning. And in addition to all these technical problems there are the important ones of sound. Some pianos have a harsh, brittle sound, because the felt that covers the hammers has become ridged and hard over the years; some pianos have a powerful, rich bass but a treble range not full and bright enough to match it. The length of the piano string is determined by the size of the piano, and the longer the string, the more resonant the sound. The standard concert grand, called a D, is nine feet long. But not infrequently a B, or seven-foot, piano is the only one available. And sometimes a pianist gets an instrument that is so close to perfect in every respect—the best Steinway, an old Mason-Hamlin in mint condition, a perfect Bechstein—that he will talk about it for months afterward.

The market for pianists is limited. If they do not succeed on the concert stage—or, as is more likely, do not even get a chance to try—they cannot fit into an orchestra, as string players can, or into an opera company, as singers can. Often, they turn to teaching, and help to produce a new batch of pianists with the same goal in mind that they themselves have failed to achieve, and thus they contribute another disadvantage—a field that is even more crowded.

If a pianist has high hopes about his chances for success, being admitted to Juilliard is bound, at first, to fortify his feelings. Everything about the place lends an air of importance to the students there. The building—part of the Lincoln Center complex—at Broadway and Sixty-sixth Street, is beautiful and opulent. The marble-floored reception area alone, on the ground floor, is vast enough to accommodate the entire corps de ballet of four or five major ballet companies, all doing their pliés and entrechats. Behind a broad polished-wood reception desk sit two people: a gracious elderly woman with a phenomenal memory for faces, who keeps an eye on everybody who comes in through the double glass doors, on Sixty-sixth Street, to make sure that no one gets in who doesn't belong there; and next to her a uniformed guard, who is there for the protection of the students and also of the valuable instruments that many of them play. The building, a five-story marble structure that covers almost half a city block, has wall-to-wall carpeting everywhere, and there are ample practice rooms and rehearsal halls, spacious studios for the faculty members, a perfect jewel of a theatre for the school's opera and modern-dance productions and its four orchestras' concerts, and an attractive, comfortable auditorium, Paul Hall, for the students' solo recitals. The school also has the use of Alice Tully Hall, which is in the southeast corner of the Juilliard building, for weekly student chamber-music concerts and performances by the school's orchestras.

Of the eight hundred or so students at Juilliard, about two hundred are pianists, and, according to Joseph Bloch, who teaches courses in piano literature there, and in whose classes have sat such pianists as Garrick Ohlsson, Van Cliburn, Misha Dichter, and John Browning, every one of the piano students hopes to become a concert artist. I asked Bloch recently how many of the current two hundred he felt had what it took to succeed. After thinking for a minute, he said, "Oh, twenty-five, twenty." Then he laughed and added, "But bear in mind that I'm the only one at Juilliard who said Van Cliburn would never have a career, and I even had my doubts about Garrick Ohlsson."

Bloch, an attractive, energetic man in his mid-fifties, who is called Jim or Jimmy by his family and friends, tried for a performing career himself when he came to New York from Indianapolis, where he was born. He made his début in Town Hall in 1950 and got favorable reviews. In those days, there were seven daily newspapers in Manhattan, and a performer could count on five or six reviews—enough to make or break him if they were strong in either direction. Bloch had become friends with Virgil Thomson, the American composer and critic, and Thomson suggested that if he gave a New York recital every year for five years something good might come of it. In 1951, Bloch, presenting his second recital, geared his program to please the critics who had reviewed him before—picked composers they were known to like. But he got different critics and ambiguous reviews, and he abandoned Thomson's five-year plan. Instead of continuing to assault the music fortress that is New York, he toured in the United States, Europe, New Zealand, Australia, and Japan in the fifties and sixties. He began teaching at Juilliard in 1948, and has been a visiting professor at schools in Hong Kong, Singapore, New Zealand, Korea, and Japan. In addition, he has played in such disparate places as Colorado and Calcutta, Taiwan and Tahiti. Bloch has also given several New York recitals since the 1951 disappointment, but his pleasure in music, travel, and a good life seems to preclude the fanaticism necessary for a major concert artist's career.

Although Bloch's piano-literature classes are required, his students consider themselves lucky to be in them. He is a storehouse of knowledge about different periods, composers, and styles, and the classes, always informative and often intense, are enjoyable and sometimes exhilarating. He is a warm, compassionate man, outside the private teacher-pupil relationship in music, which, emotionally, can be similar to that between parent and child, or analyst and analysand, and can be extremely painful and trying. Piano students like to play their recital program for him— or, at least, a certain piece—because his advice on fine points of interpretation is invaluable.

I asked Bloch why he had had reservations about Cliburn, and he said, "He auditioned here when he was sixteen, and he played the Liszt Twelfth Hungarian Rhapsody so beautifully I still remember it vividly. But as the years went by and I watched his progress, it seemed to me that he had no intellectual curiosity about piano repertoire, and I felt that that would be a severe handicap to a career."

"And Ohlsson?" I asked.

Bloch said, "He had a formidable technique and a profound intellectual curiosity about piano literature. But he was quiet—almost markedly reserved—and I felt his personality might be a handicap. Audiences like to feel a warmth emanating from the stage—some like to talk to the artists after the concert. I felt Garrick's reserve would put them off." He laughed and added, "You can see how wrong I was. Garrick won three big competitions in a row—including the Chopin—and his personality is blossoming along with his career. He's now outgoing and approachable."

Chapter

2

I first became interested in the problems of student pianists, and how they go about trying for a career, in the fall of 1973, when I met Robin McCabe, one of Juilliard's two hundred. Juilliard has no dormitory facilities, and a pupil from out of town either pairs up with another student to rent an apartment or lives in a residential hotel or takes a room with kitchen privileges in a private apartment—preferably somewhere in the vicinity of Juilliard. Robin and another Juilliard pianist, Richard Fields, each rented a room in the duplex apartment of Jane Harris, a pianist friend of mine who lived off Central Park West two blocks north of the school. I lived in the same building, and sometimes caught glimpses of Robin—usually on the run. She spent her days at the school—from eight in the morning, when it opens, until ten at night, when it closes. Sundays, when it is locked for the day, were spent in a frantic search for a piano to practice on. I rarely saw Richard. Pianists come to Juilliard to study with a particular teacher or they take their chances, but, once they have been assigned to a teacher, they are committed. Changing teachers—especially in mid-year—requires a strong ego and the tact of a diplomat; the student must find another teacher who is willing to take him at the risk of alienating the current teacher, and must get a release from the current teacher, who may feel well rid of him but angered or embarrassed at what might appear to be a public rebuke. Richard was a shy young man, and a talented pianist. A pre-school student at the New England Conservatory, in Boston, where he grew up, he'd come to Juilliard fresh from high school —he was younger than Robin—and he was unhappy with his teacher, who overwhelmed him in general and verbally scalded him when he did not live up to her expectations. Richard frequently slept half the day away in escape from the trauma awaiting him at school.

Robin and Richard used the upstairs door of Jane's apartment, and sometimes when I was there Robin would come downstairs to tell us something funny that had happened at school or talk about a concert she was going to give. She was one of two pupils of the brilliant Czech pianist Rudolf Firkusny, and one of eight students in Juilliard's new doctoral program. Robin is a beautiful girl, with green eyes, high cheekbones, a soft, perfect complexion, and black curly hair that frames her face and touches her shoulders. At the time I met her, she wore demure dresses that her mother bought for her, and looked more like a Katharine Gibbs secretary than like a talented, many-faceted musician. When she smiled, which was often, there was a sparkle in her eyes, and when she laughed her cheeks dimpled, though her face in repose sometimes looked sad.

One night in the spring of 1974, I ran into Robin on the street. Her cheeks were pink after a fast sprint from school, where she had been practicing. I hadn't seen her in some time, and I asked how things were going. She said, "I'm competing in the Concert Artists Guild competition right now, and the finals are tomorrow. After that, I'll tell you." As it turned out, she was a winner. Each year, the Concert Artists Guild awards up to ten first prizes of a New York début in Carnegie Recital Hall to an assortment of string players, singers, ensembles (woodwinds, strings, or brass), and one or two pianists. The year Robin entered, there were, in the opinion of the judges, few string players—and no violinists—ready for a début recital. As a result, the Guild chose four piano winners from a field of eighty-one: Robin; Alan Weiss, who was Firkusny's other pupil; Gary Steigerwalt, a third Juilliard student, who was a pupil of Irwin Freundlich; and David Northington, from Yale University. In many cases, the judges—six well-known pianists and a critic for *High Fidelity*, Harris Goldsmith—simply wrote "Yes" or "No" in commenting on the performances; sometimes they went into detail about what they thought of each contestant's playing. Robin was happy to see not only that the judges' "Yes"es for her were unanimous— many with exclamation marks—but also that Goldsmith, whose opinion she especially valued, on the basis of his record reviews, had written about her, "Yes! A true performer, plays with strength and distinction. Good pedal. Clearly focused. Ravel: Intense and mysterious. Chopin played in grand manner. Falla: Huge crescendos brilliantly done, rhythmic tension even in the face of technical complexities." However, when it came time for what Bloch calls the "horsetrading," Goldsmith's vote went to Alan Weiss. Goldsmith said he felt Robin was not quite ready for a big career, though not even the Concert Artists Guild would claim that winning that contest was a launching pad for instant stardom. It's a good competition, an honest one, but geared more to be a stepping stone toward the long climb ahead. Robin's début was set for April 1, 1975, and Alan's for January 7th of the same year.

After the competition, I managed to talk to Robin several times and learn something about her background. No one is busier or less accessible than serious music students. They are either in a class or practicing. And Robin, while working hard at Juilliard, was trying to support herself. She had decided after she graduated from college to accept as little money as possible from her parents, although she always knew that if she really needed help, they would give it. She felt that they had already done enough for her, and, besides, they had two other daughters to see through school.

Robin taught Thursday afternoons at the Harlem School of the Arts, at St. Nicholas Avenue and 141st Street. She also got lots of nonclassical playing jobs. She had always been able to play by ear, and, through her ease at the piano and her thorough familiarity with chord structure and harmony, had evolved a wonderful style with popular music

—something she calls soft jazz. The student-services office at Juilliard was sometimes asked for the name of a student who could play popular music, and the office would often recommend Robin. She had played at a number of consulate parties and at a birthday party for Senator Jacob Javits, and as word spread she began to get almost more work than she could handle. She once told me that while she was playing on such occasions she every now and then found herself thinking that maybe no one would give her nearly as much—or anything—for playing a Beethoven sonata.

In June of 1971, when Robin was twenty-one, she came to New York from Puyallup, Washington, a small town near Seattle, to audition for admission to Juilliard's graduate program. She had just graduated summa cum laude from the University of Washington, in Seattle, where she had majored in music. Béla Siki, her piano teacher there, had suggested the move to New York. Robin had already achieved considerable success as a pianist in the Northwest; she had won almost every regional competition she entered, and had given a number of recitals. (Siki, who was born in Budapest in 1923, had studied with Ernst von Dohnányi and become the protégé of the Rumanian pianist Dinu Lipatti. When Lipatti, one of Europe's great pianists and the nonpareil interpreter of Chopin, died tragically at the age of thirty-three, Siki took charge of his students. Now, in addition to teaching in Washington, he tours Europe annually, giving solo recitals and performing with orchestras.) Siki told Robin that for a serious musician New York was the only place from which to approach a career. Also, Robin knew that, because of the vast number of musicians in every country and the intensely competitive nature of the business, very few can make a living out of performing alone; almost every artist is affiliated with a school and teaches at least part time. In recent years, schools have begun to require advanced degrees of their performing faculty members, and a degree from Juilliard carries a lot of weight.

Robin is the oldest of three daughters, and the family is an especially close one. Her father, Dr. Edward McCabe, provided a home verging on the opulent that was comfortable and homey, decorated with care and taste by Robin's mother, Lou. Childhood photographs of Robin and her family reflect an environment that many child psychologists would call ideal. Holidays were observed with obvious warmth and joy, the dinner table often enlarged to include relatives and friends.

Snapshots of Robin at age two show her sitting on the lawn, reading, watched over by an interested black German shepherd named Cinders. The second daughter, Rachelle, was born when Robin was six, but for those first years Robin had her parents all to herself, and there are scenes of Robin with her father, standing on the dock at Spirit Lake, Idaho, where the McCabes have a summer home; Robin is wearing a large straw hat and holding a string of the day's catch. Robin at three, with her new red wagon, grinning from ear to ear. Two years later, the same smile and a new bicycle, with training wheels. Robin at six, on her first skis, at Sun Valley with her parents. (Robin's father taught all the girls to ski, swim, dive, and play tennis.) Robin in a Halloween costume—an ambivalent black-and-white tiger—holding a pumpkin. Robin, eleven, and Chelle (Rachelle's nickname, pronounced Shelley), five, sitting on the diving board of the pool behind the family home. (Renée was born the following year.) Mrs. McCabe loves flowers, and in the summer the vast manicured lawn is beautifully bordered with an artful assortment. Trellises near the house are laden with her favorite—roses. And there are several snapshots of Robin at the piano, with her first teacher, Kay Logan, a matronly, warm-looking woman, sitting next to her.

Dr. and Mrs. McCabe each played the piano—although neither with any real skill—and when Robin was still a toddler she liked to pick out tunes on the piano, and they taught her the names of the keys. One evening, Mrs. McCabe was preparing dinner, with Robin in attendance, and Dr. McCabe was playing the piano. He hit a wrong note and Robin, now five, called out, "E-*flat!*" It was then that they discovered she had perfect pitch, and soon after they took her to Kay Logan, who was her teacher for the next nine years.

Robin says that at first she enjoyed lessons and practicing. Mrs. Logan taught in the home of an elderly woman, who was fond of Robin. Robin says, "I remember a dress I wore. It was red, with little pockets all around the waist, and this woman would fill the pockets with candy every time I went for a lesson." It was expected at home that she would practice several hours a day, but when she was eleven she began to feel rebellious about it. Thursday was her father's day off, and her parents went skiing or played tennis, depending on the weather. Robin recalls, "I'd put lots of music out on the piano, and I would work for fifteen minutes. My little sister was there, and she couldn't tell time. After fifteen minutes of practice, I'd say, 'Oh, wow, I'm really tired. I really worked hard,' and I'd quit. Then we'd have an absolute orgy of self-indulgence, eating ice cream and watching television. And when my parents came home, Chelle would say, 'Oh, Robin practiced a *long* time,' echoing me. They never *forced* me to practice, though my mother would gently nudge me. 'Aren't you going to practice?' I was excused from dishes and housework, and usually practiced after school, before I did my homework."

Robin was a straight-A student through grade school, high school, and college. She says that throughout her school years she was usually in fierce competition with one or two other girls over high marks, and the rivalry wasn't always friendly. "Children are sometimes shockingly cruel," she observes now. She was often called on to play at school assemblies and remembers feeling a bit apart from her peers, though not an outcast. She dated the school superintendent's son in high school, and her classmates thought that that was appropriate. She says, "When I was a senior in high school, I ran for student-body secretary. That was my big bid for everybody's acceptance. And I really wanted it. I was active in school affairs, and I guess I felt winning would make me a real high-school jock— popular—but I lost to a girl whose father was also a doctor. I was very upset. We'd grown up together and we'd skied together, and we were rivals. She was everything that I felt I wasn't—very gregarious and very blond and very charming, a gay, effervescent person, which I was not."

Robin says she didn't take piano very seriously until the summer she was thirteen. "My mother drove me to the University of Washington for what we both thought was a piano seminar. You know, I would play and get constructive criticism. But it was a competition, and I won, and my little ego just skyrocketed. It was not the prize so much as being told, 'You are the best.' At that age, I only dimly

[23]

knew what a concert artist was. Once, my mother took me to Seattle to hear Iturbi, and I thought he was something great, though, in truth, I would rather have gone to a movie."

After teaching Robin for nine years, Mrs. Logan suggested that the McCabes find another teacher for her—that Robin had outgrown her, become too advanced—and that there was nothing more she could teach her. Robin was playing pieces that she now realizes were above her level. "I was using clout to get through them. Forcing, and generally not being very good, not fastidious. I played a lot of pieces kind of ramrodding my way through. The clarity was not good. In one respect it was valuable at that age, because even though the pieces were beyond me, I got my first acquaintance with them. And the man I went to after Mrs. Logan said, 'Wow—I'm going to have to be a real policeman with you.' I'm grateful to Mrs. Logan. I don't think it was an easy thing for her to do—to give me up—and my parents would never have taken the initiative."

Robin adjusted easily to the University of Washington. Although the enrollment was forty thousand, the music department was like a small community, and Béla Siki, her teacher throughout her four years there, was and remains a hero to her. Robin lived in a dorm and didn't try for a sorority because she felt it would be too time consuming. Unlike many music students, she got deeply involved in other subjects—art history, literature, French, and, for a while, economics. She comments, "I often wonder what effect the sidetracking might have had on my playing—if my piano technique suffered a great deal in the process."

Siki guided Robin through the piano repertoire, knowing that in order to begin a career she would have to have in her fingers certain basic pieces, and it had been immediately clear to him that to be a concert pianist was her goal. (It might eventually be Rachelle's and Renée's goal, too. Mrs. McCabe started both of them on piano when they reached the age of five.)

When Robin came to New York for the audition, she knew no one in the city. A local travel agent naïvely suggested a West Side hotel near Juilliard. It was a rundown, shabby, depressing place, but Robin, not knowing where else to go, stayed there. She admits to having been acutely lonely. The audition was brief and, she felt, very cold. "You play for seven members of the piano faculty," she told me. "They let you play about fifteen minutes at the most, and it's all chopped up. They interrupt and ask to hear parts of different pieces, and then you're dismissed with 'Thank you. You'll be hearing from us.' You are given theory exams, but I've since learned that they're purely for placement. Someone who couldn't draw a treble clef would still get in if he played well enough. The Juilliard faculty members are interested in raw talent. If you're deficient in theory, they'll give you remedial counterpoint and so on. But the audition is everything." During the three days Robin was in New York, she took in as many tourist attractions as she could—the Empire State Building, the Statue of Liberty, the Staten Island ferry—reasoning that if she wasn't accepted at Juilliard it would be her last chance for a long time to see the city.

Robin received word late in June that she had been accepted, and she returned in the fall and stayed at the Y until she found a room, in the West Nineties. She was almost overwhelmed by Juilliard at first—it was so big; the teachers, many of them concert artists, seemed formidable; and the number and quality of the students made her have severe doubts about herself. For a while, she was ambivalent about even considering a career. She told me one day, "I just thought, Please, God, let me get my degree and I'll leave, I promise. I'll get out. No static." (Robin grew up a Catholic, and she occasionally makes references to her religion and frequently, half kiddingly, speaks directly to God.) Now she laughed at the memory. "I felt like such a transplant. I knew that I was up against a tremendous current of people who were already in the mainstream— and New York *is* the musical mainstream. I didn't even have any contacts. I felt that if I could get a degree, at least I wouldn't have wasted a lot of money. For a couple of months, I was terribly intimidated and homesick. I walked around school not daring to talk to anyone." She paused for a few seconds, and went on, "I had an incredible experience my first month at school. I was practicing one day, and a man came into my room and asked if I was a student there. I thought, Oh, my God, I sound so bad he thinks I don't even *go* to Juilliard. I told him I was, and he left. I found out much later that he was the piano technician, and that it was his habit to check on new faces. It seems funny now, but at the time it really upset me."

Robin thinks of the piano students at Juilliard as falling into three categories—big guns, medium-sized guns, and little guns—and during her first two years there she definitely considered herself one of the little guns. Partly from shyness and partly from a lifelong habit of hard work, she made few friends at first and concentrated on piano. She studied with the teacher whom Béla Siki had recommended

—Ilona Kabos. Robin said of her, "She was Hungarian, and an excellent teacher, though she was extremely tempestuous. She used to scream at me—lots of Hungarian histrionics—but she was good for me. She liked my playing but felt I needed more chutzpah—needed to come out more. She pushed me quite a bit. I remember one lesson in particular. It was a hot spring day. I was playing the last measures of the Liszt A-Major Concerto. There are tremendous, blazing octave passages—*very* hard. The heat bothered me, my hair was falling in my face, and I was flubbing a lot of notes. I finally said, 'I don't know what's wrong with me. I keep missing it. It's so dirty, messy,' and she said, '*Dar*ling, really, if you would just lean back and get your bosom out of the way.'" Robin laughed. "She was right. I was leaning too far forward." She added, "Mme. Kabos often told me she was disappointed in me—she was often very rough on me. I was highly demolishable at the time, and I don't think she knew how much she hurt me. I would go back to my room and beat myself mentally. But it would be better the next time. In the middle of my second year, she got very sick. We didn't know it at the time, but it was cancer. She returned to her home in London, and we all knew, somehow, that she wouldn't be back. I felt awfully depressed about it, and for a while I didn't study with anyone. But then I heard that Firkusny was coming back to Juilliard—he had taught there years ago—and was going to take two pupils. Siki knew Firkusny and recommended me, and I'll always be grateful. He's a wonderful person—much softer than Mme. Kabos. He arouses a tremendous conscience in a student. Without saying that something is wretched, he says, 'This could be better,' and you know that in his understated way he's saying, 'This is really lacking. You'd better get going and show me something better.' But he can be articulate, concrete, and very, very helpful." Her thoughts returned to Mme. Kabos, and she said, "She was a great lady—a *grande dame*, in the tradition of Rosina Lhevinne and Ania Dorfmann. She is very much missed."

Chapter
3

Competitions have become an important part of every young musician's life—to have a career it's almost essential that he win at least one. In the fall of 1972, before returning to Juilliard from a summer of teaching at the University of Washington and lessons with Siki, Robin entered the Twenty-eighth Geneva Concours International, at Siki's suggestion. Almost every country in Europe has its own *concours,* and Siki picked the one in Geneva for Robin because he had friends there she could stay with. Robin had competed many times in the Northwest, but this was to be the first time on an international scale; the rules would be different and the competition, needless to say, much stiffer. The Geneva Concours admits contestants on the basis of what Robin calls "propaganda"—contests won, teachers studied with, letters of recommendation from music-department chairmen. Some competitions require a tape from the contestant, but the Geneva does not. All have specific repertoire requirements, and the Geneva's were ninety minutes of solo playing, including works representative of the Baroque, classic, Romantic, and modern periods. No competition is for the nervous or the squeamish. Contestants in the Geneva preliminaries and the semifinals are rarely permitted to finish anything they start. They are constantly being interrupted by the judges —a panel of the best pianists that the competition can get —and asked to play something else. Thus, they leap from composer to composer, from period to period, hoping to communicate something—to convey some degree of musicianship and technique. At the Geneva, the judges sat behind a curtain for the first round, and the pianists were given numbers. Blind judging is standard procedure in many contests—to keep the competition honest—but Robin found it unnerving. She said, "They sit behind this big green curtain. Not only that, when you come out to play—this big preliminary you've traveled thousands of miles for—they won't let you warm up with scales. Everyone is given the same piece to play. They fear that a contestant might start with a four-octave B-major scale in thirds, say, and it could be a signal to a judge. I have to admit, though, that when everyone plays the same piece it can be very telling."

Robin said that at first she felt almost paralyzed with fear. The number assigned her was 33, and she made the association that it was appropriate because Christ was crucified when he was thirty-three. Now she laughs at the connection—calls it all her Catholic guilt coming out. She said, "During the preliminaries, we were waiting backstage, and there was a Yugoslavian boy who had brought along a portable silent keyboard with a weight attached to each key, to regulate the action. He was sitting there in front of all us victims, a cigarette hanging out of his mouth, and he was practicing madly. It was *so* disconcerting. I wished I had one, too. I saw him afterward and asked him how it went, and he said glumly, 'It didn't.' And he was right—he didn't get past the preliminaries. Sometimes you just know. You can have a memory slip and not make a quick recovery, and you know you're washed up—you've had it."

There were about ninety-five pianists at the Geneva Concours. The judges narrowed the field to twenty, and then to ten. Second, third, and fourth prizes were awarded, but no first. Robin was the only American among the ten finalists—a Concours laureate. She was pleased but not elated, and, typically, went in search of criticism of her playing, so that she could profit from the experience. She was told that one judge did not like her Beethoven; he said that it had an American accent. She said to me, "Now, that's a comment that I think is absolutely meaningless. It doesn't help me at all. I came away not knowing what was really wrong. I have an inkling that he meant I didn't play in the German *Sturm und Drang* style—you know, *heavy, heavy*. I do know that every one of the judges was European. There wasn't one American." The prizes for the laureates were

[31]

recitals in Victoria Hall, in Geneva, and after Robin's recital *Le Journal* said of her, in part, "Excellent pianism . . . and a sensitive, beautifully revealed musicianship."

Memory slips are the bane of many performers, and I asked Robin if they were a problem for her.

She said, "I've had a few, but not in a long time. I had one once during a concert in Spokane. Somebody in the first row took a picture of me. I was playing the Beethoven 'Waldstein' Sonata, and the flash broke my concentration and I was gone—lost. So I improvised for what seemed like twenty minutes but was closer to twenty seconds, and then I found my place again. After the concert, my mother said it sounded like Debussy and Gershwin. I'm not sure anyone else even noticed, but it upset me so much I threw up. That was the last time it happened to me, but I'm still aware of the danger.

"One time, I played the Schumann Concerto in A Minor with a Canadian orchestra. The concerto starts with a unison E in the orchestra, and the piano enters with a dramatic rapid chordal passage. I went onstage, adjusted the piano bench, and sat for a moment, to compose myself. We'd had two rehearsals, and I was ready. There was a large audience, and suddenly I couldn't remember the very first chord. I blanked out—mistrusted everything. I thought, Oh, my God, I don't even know where to *begin.* I wiped the keys with my handkerchief, tried to look busy. The conductor was watching me, and I was having a total coronary. I imagined that the audience was getting restless. Finally, my mind completely blank, I nodded to the conductor to begin. I heard the orchestra E, and my hands went for the right chord. Total intuition, and I was all right. But if I had tried to intellectualize I would still be sitting there."

Robin told me about another concert in Canada—different concerto, different orchestra. "I did the Saint-Saëns Concerto No. 2 in G Minor. It starts out with solo piano. The orchestra doesn't come in for a minute or so. The piano part begins with an emphatic octave leading into a grandiose, romantic theme. The hall was huge and almost filled. The conductor nodded to me to start. I struck the octave and the piano rolled away from me. I moved the stool forward and tried to keep playing, but the piano moved again. It was on a dolly, and there was a slight incline in the stage." She shrugged helplessly. "I didn't know what to do. I looked at the conductor, and he had his hand over his mouth. The concertmaster had his bow across his face. The hall was pin-dropping quiet. I looked out at the audience and started to laugh, and then everyone laughed—roared. A stagehand came out and put blocks under the rollers. The next day, the critic couldn't resist calling it 'A Moving Performance.' "

Robin's first doctoral recital—she would give three such recitals all told, within the next two years—was scheduled for May 17, 1974, in Paul Hall, and immediately after the Concert Artists Guild competition she began serious work on her recital program. On May 8th, Bloch arranged for her and the two other C.A.G. winners from the school to play for Everett Lee, the newly appointed conductor of the Symphony of the New World, at Juilliard. The symphony gave a series of four concerts in Avery Fisher Hall each year, and Lee was looking for a young soloist. The opportunity to play with an orchestra in a big hall in New York is every young artist's dream—second only to having a manager—and Robin interrupted work on her recital to spend a couple of hours polishing the Rachmaninoff Rhapsody on a Theme of Paganini. It was solidly in her repertoire, but she had not played it for several months. She had thought of skipping the playoff—it might be a waste of time —but it seemed too big a chance to pass up.

Bloch had invited me to listen, and he met me at the Juilliard reception desk at four o'clock. As usual, he moved through the school at a half trot, but, with recitals coming up, he was stopped frequently by students who would tug at his sleeve or stand in his way to ask, "Mr. Bloch, can you hear my Bach before next week?" or "Will you listen to my Mozart?" or "Can I play the Bartók for you?" He told each of them to get in touch with him the next day. The audition for Lee was to be held in Bloch's studio, on the fifth floor. The conductor had not arrived, and Bloch led me into the studio next to his, and introduced me to Ania Dorfmann, and then went outside to wait for Lee.

Mme. Dorfmann, one of Juilliard's best teachers, had a successful career as a concert pianist—a rarity for a woman some years ago. She was one of the few women asked by Toscanini to appear as soloist with his symphony, and their recording of the Beethoven First Concerto is a collectors' item. Some people feel that the conductor was challenging the soloist and that she more than met the challenge, with the result that the last movement is taken at a precedent-setting speed. In her studio there are a number of autographed photographs of famous musicians—handsomely framed and mounted on pedestals—including several of Toscanini. Mme. Dorfmann, who was born in Russia in 1899, is a petite, stunning woman with piercing sapphire-blue eyes that seem to miss nothing. She is quick-witted and fast to speak, and often, according to some of her students, she can be very cutting. She undoubtedly has reason to be. Mme. Dorfmann gives her life to teaching, and she has much to offer her pupils, but some of them, for various, often emotional, reasons, don't respond and make the progress she feels they can and hopes they will.

Mme. Dorfmann was a chain smoker until recently, and she was smoking when I met her. In a few minutes, she said, she would be going down to the Juilliard Theatre to help judge a concerto contest. Four or five times a year, Juilliard piano students compete to play a specific concerto with the school's orchestras. Mme. Dorfmann said, "It won't take long this time. There are only three pianists, because the concerto is the Prokofieff Second—very difficult. Last time, the concerto was the Chopin F Minor, and there were eighteen. One of my pupils is playing today. He will not win." She put her cigarette out, lit another, and added dryly, "He should not. My pupils always want to play what the other one is playing. What is in the other basket always looks better."

Bloch now beckoned to me from the doorway. Lee had arrived, he told me, and the playoff would begin. Out in the hall, sitting on the floor, talking and laughing and looking like three young men relaxing after a game of touch football, were Alan Weiss, Gary Steigerwalt, and James Barbagallo, a pianist who would play the orchestra parts for the three contestants. Barbagallo is a handsome, engaging young man, and Bloch had told me that he had a promising future—that he was a big talent. Inside Bloch's studio, which has two Steinway grands facing each other and two rows of chairs for his piano-literature classes, were Lee and Martin Canin, a member of the piano faculty. Alan played a movement from the Brahms Second Concerto, and Gary did a movement of a Mozart concerto. Robin, looking drawn and pale and tired, was last. Lee, as he had with the others, asked her to tell him something about herself. She smiled and said, "I brought you a copy of my propaganda." She handed it to him and said, "I know you're very busy, so we've worked out a fifteen-minute capsule of the Rachmaninoff. If we leave out any of your favorite variations, just tell us, and we'll be happy to do them for you." The Rachmaninoff was the most romantic, dramatic music played that afternoon, and Robin did it with power, intensity, and obvious love. She was the first to get applause from Canin and Bloch, and Lee, applauding, said, "Bravo! Bravo!"

After Robin left, Lee said that all three had played well but that he would have liked to hear Gary do something other than the Mozart. (The composer whom many people consider the greatest of them all can sound tame sandwiched between two lusher works, though not, one would think, to a conductor.) It turned out that Lee intended to hear a number of string players and singers who had won other competitions, and he told Bloch that he would be in touch with him. Eventually, I learned, Lee chose a sixteen-year-old pianist from New Jersey whom he had heard of by word of mouth.

I was interested in learning something about Alan Weiss, Firkusny's other pupil, and after saying goodbye to Bloch, I met Alan in the cafeteria. He is a slight, intense young man with short curly hair and wire-rimmed glasses. Over coffee, he talked about his life. His career in music began at the age of nine, when he started on classical guitar. Within a year, he was so accomplished that a family friend arranged an audition for Alan with Segovia, to seek the master's evaluation of Alan's talent. It was Alan's father who wanted his son to be a musician. The father is an amateur violinist—a very good one, according to Alan—who got lessons in Poland, where he was a watchmaker, in exchange for teaching his violin teacher's two sons the craft he knew so well.

"My father thought I was very talented, but then all parents think that of their children." Alan told me that he loved to practice, to the extent that he could resist his friends' calling from the back yard, "Butchie, come play kick ball." He was tempted, though, because he also loved to play kick ball. His friends teased him about his music, but not mercilessly, he says.

Segovia told Alan he should also study piano, because it would provide a good base for theory, and he referred Alan to Gustavo Lopez, a former assistant of his, for guitar lessons. The Weiss family lived in Waterbury, Connecticut, and every Saturday Alan's father drove him to New York for a guitar lesson. Alan took piano lessons in Waterbury from a woman named Ava Grossman, who, Alan says, "was absolutely fantastic and inspiring for me." He studied both instruments for two years, though it was difficult. Long nails on the right hand are essential for a guitarist and disastrous for a pianist. Mrs. Grossman hoped he would become totally dedicated to piano, and in time he did. He said, "I think I reached some kind of saturation point with guitar. The repertoire is quite limited, which is certainly not true of piano. I felt bad for my father. He thought the field for guitarists was much less crowded, and I'd have a better chance of a career if I stuck to that instrument."

Alan began studying piano in Juilliard's pre-school division with Beveridge Webster, a renowned concert artist. When I met Alan, he had been at Juilliard for nine years, had completed work on his master's degree, and was about to begin work on his doctorate.

Alan was ambivalent about Juilliard during his early years there. "I had a great deal of difficulty adjusting to Juilliard and learning where my own gifts lay in regard to music." In Waterbury, he had spent most of his free time listening to records of the world's great pianists, and he said, "I used to be intolerant when I was seventeen or so. I was bursting with energy, and I didn't like anyone's playing—including my own—except for the truly great, and it's unrealistic, because when you grow older you have to accept yourself as you are, and if you're not a Horowitz or a Schnabel . . . Well, you can't commit suicide." Alan studied with Webster for three years in pre-college and two years in college, and he recalls, "The first three years were magnificent and the next two were a complete disaster, partly because I didn't pay heed to what he said. And I was very rude to him. Looking back, I realize I absolutely idolized him during the first years. I put him on such a pedestal I was bound to become disillusioned, and unfortunately I did. I think I see things with a little bit more clarity now. He was wonderful for my musical growth and creativity, but I felt he did not pay enough attention to technical problems, and as a result I myself did not concentrate enough on technique." He summed up his years with Webster thus: "He's a great musician who gave everything he could to me. I'm afraid all I gave him was a lot of grief and a lot of problems."

For the next three years, Alan went through the painful discipline of repressing his creative side and working on technical problems exclusively—a boring diet for a young man exuding the joy of music. He told me, "I tried to completely divorce my technical thinking from my musical thinking, and now I realize it was very dangerous. I was being pulled in opposite directions. I know now that one must follow one's artistic convictions and derive the technique from the art, rather than the other way around." At this time, Juilliard gave him a fellowship in the Secondary Division, teaching students whose major instrument might be violin or cello but who were required to study piano, too, for three years. Alan said that in the process of teaching others the proper way to play scales and arpeggios he learned a lot himself. The head of the department, Frances Goldstein, was another one of his heroes. "She's one of the most inspiring human beings. An incredible person. And even though I was not her pupil, she was very helpful in making me see my shortcomings. She has such clear-sightedness. You can't escape her vision."

Alan and Robin both studied with Ilona Kabos, and Alan said it was hard for him to take criticism, especially the scathing kind Mme. Kabos was famous for. "We fought like cats and dogs—she wanted to throw me out of her class. For the first two years, it was sheer torture, though I have to admit she really pulled me together—especially the third year I studied with her. No matter how stormy she was, she would always say things for the benefit of the student, not to show off. Sometimes there was the element of her being the queen, but she always tried to extract from me what was there to extract. Through it all, I learned a great deal from her." After Mme. Kabos's death, Alan auditioned for Firkusny and was accepted. Alan felt one of his problems had always been the fact that he took instructions in the scores too literally, and he believes Firkusny has been a tremendous help in teaching him to overcome this form of rigidity, possibly an inevitable reaction to all the records he listened to. But he observed, "I think probably, in the end, the more one hears the more one learns from everybody, and the more one naturally synthesizes certain things. It's very dangerous to consciously imitate somebody's interpretation, even if you admire him very much. For instance, when Schnabel plays I get the feeling I've never gotten from any other pianist of this unbelievable, almost centrifugal force—that the music is a living organism you can feel. Rhythmically, Schnabel holds the piece together so that you feel the line, the shape, the organic unity. The tensions and the releases within him, his understanding of what he's playing, his joy in playing it are incredible. And, of course, if I thought about a Beethoven piece I've heard him play while I'm playing it, it would be totally devastating to me, so I have to kind of put on blinders."

Alan said of Mr. Firkusny, who seemed to be the first teacher at Juilliard whom he truly connected with, "He's not one of those teachers who scream and holler to get their point across. He's genial by nature, and I pay more attention to him than I do to someone who's trying to shove something down my throat. It all depends upon the student, I suppose. I respond more to suggestion. There's great integrity and conviction behind his musical thought. He's a great pianist and musician; he's not a full-time teacher, and perhaps he thinks, 'If a student comes to me, it's because he wants to learn what I feel about music, and what I have to say about technique and interpretation,' and, as far as I'm concerned, if a student doesn't want to take what he can get from a lesson—well, that's the student's tough luck."

Alan added that Mr. Firkusny was helping him overcome his "damned literalness." He said, "Another benefit of studying with a performing artist is that he can explain what he wants, and demonstrate it so that you can hear exactly what he means. He helped me with the Schubert Sonata in D Major, one of the works I played at the competition—one of the most magical pieces. I was working on a section of the slow movement, a very gentle, lovely part, and with his incredible finesse he played it for me, and it sounded like golden drops of honey shining in the sun. I was stunned, and he said, 'You can play it like that.' I said, 'I can't play it like that, but I can strive for it.'"

After getting his master's degree, Alan spent a year just taking lessons. He had applied to Juilliard's doctoral program, but he was not accepted because he didn't have enough performing experience—a result, he says, of the fact that he had so little confidence in himself. He said that the troubled five years he'd had, starting when he was seventeen, had set him back, though he added, "Of course, my troubles are far from over."

He had gone to Aspen several summers, and in June would go to Marlboro, the chamber-music camp for professionals and advanced students. "I'm looking forward to the chamber-music experience—I haven't had a lot—and at the same time I'm terrified. I have five big pieces to learn in a month, and the caliber of performance and the competition there must be horrendous." He had given a number of concerts during the year that qualified him for the doctoral program, which he would begin in the fall.

Alan shared an apartment with another pianist, and the previous year he had met a girl at school—Makiko Sakai, a Japanese pianist—and the two had become inseparable. Some of Alan's peers feared the relationship might hamper his career, interfere with his hard work. But Alan clearly felt buoyed by her, and happier in his work. There aren't too many light-hearted moments at Juilliard, and everyone, including Alan, enjoyed this one: Two piano students were eavesdropping outside Paul Hall. Someone was practicing, and the two were trying to figure out who it was. One said to the other, "It must be Makiko. I just saw Alan, and he was alone."

Before we parted, I said, "It seems to me the one thing you young musicians have in common is great courage."

For the first time, Alan laughed. He said, "Either that or great stupidity. I think what happens is that when you're young your parents don't really know how difficult the field is and what has to be done. One not only has to be very gifted in music but very intelligent, responsible. You have to have a lot of drive. You have to be very self-critical, and that's difficult because in order to perform you have to be extremely self-confident. It's a tricky balance. Not many people have been able to cope with the problem successfully. You have to know your own mind and at the same time absorb incredible criticism from others. You have to be cynical and shrewd and still capable of being profoundly moved by the joy and beauty in music. It's walking a high wire, and onstage there's no net."

I left Alan and went to the practice floor—the fourth— to look for Robin. It is a labyrinth of winding corridors lined with lockers and many small rooms. I asked a young girl in bluejeans and a Beethoven sweatshirt, who was pacing up and down and shaking her arms as if to rid them of numbness, whether she knew where Robin was. She pointed down a hall and said, "All the way and turn left. She's almost always in the last room."

The practice rooms all have, in addition to wall-to-wall carpeting, heavy drapes to absorb the sound of the grand pianos. I found Robin and went in. She was working on one of her encores, the Liszt "Gnomenreigen" Étude in F Sharp. She stumbled in one passage, stopped, rapidly played an F-sharp-major four-octave scale three times, returned to the difficult passage, and played it flawlessly. I told her that she had apparently done well in the playoff. She looked pleased and said, "It was a long shot, and maybe nothing will come of it, but it was worth a try. I had some doubts about the Rachmaninoff—that truncated version— but I'm happy with how it went. Right now, I'm too tired to play one more note, so I'm going to take a break and get something to eat. Then maybe I can keep going until ten o'clock." She picked up her shoulder bag and turned off the light, and we started down the hall to the elevators. In front of us was a girl in bright horizontal-striped knee socks, no shoes, and cut-offs with "I'm Available" stenciled on the seat. She was out of earshot, and Robin told me, "She's a bit of a joke around school, but she's very talented, and just won a Fulbright that will enable her to study in Europe with a teacher of her choice."

A friend of Robin's, Roman Markowicz, popped out of a practice room and stopped us. Roman, a pupil of Mme. Dorfmann, was born in Poland and came to America when he was twenty-one. His European dress and manner give him an almost staid, stuffy appearance, which is immediately alleviated when he speaks. He greeted Robin with a gallant hand kiss. A friend of both students was performing that night in Carnegie Recital Hall, and Roman was trying to decide whether to go or to stay and practice. He, too, had a recital coming up, but he was faced with a problem: Paul Hall was solidly booked through the end of the semester, and there was no place for him to play. Robin offered to bring him coffee, but he declined. He said that he thought he would go and hear part of the recital and then come back to school to practice. There is an element of timelessness on the practice floor at Juilliard—an almost palpable seductive pull toward the piano—and it is easy to imagine that if the school did not close at ten the students would practice until they dropped.

A bulletin board next to the elevators was covered with overlapping announcements of recitals. Some were decorated with hand-painted flowers, and on several was printed, in large, colorful letters, "*Please* come!" Robin said everyone was so busy at that time of the year that no performers could expect much of a turnout beyond family and friends and, in some cases, a few faculty members. Faculty members are especially busy, and tend to go only to their own pupils' recitals and possibly one or two others when the performers are rumored to have made great progress during the year. Outside Juilliard, Robin paused to enjoy the fresh spring evening. She seemed to exist on hamburgers, and said that she had planned to go to McDonald's on Seventy-first Street but had changed her mind and would go to Smiler's, instead. It was just around the corner and wouldn't take as long.

Chapter

4

One problem that young musicians studying with pianists of the stature of Firkusny have is that their teachers are often on tour, and so it happened that Robin had made her way through the Concert Artists Guild competition and was completing work on her doctoral recital without her teacher's help. During Firkusny's absence, she had sought opinions from other pupils, and had played parts of her program—the Chopin "Funeral March" Sonata in B Flat Minor and the Beethoven Sonata in E Flat Major—for a friend of Jane Harris's, the pianist Mitchell Andrews. The rest of her program would consist of Three Burlesques of Béla Bartók; two Schubert-Liszt transcriptions; a Schumann-Liszt lieder transcription; and the entire Ravel *Miroirs*.

On Wednesday, May 15th, at eleven o'clock in the morning, Robin was to have her first lesson with Firkusny in over six weeks, and she got permission from him to let me listen. She was eager to play some of her recital pieces for him and to straighten out certain passages that had been bothering her. Her mother was coming from Puyallup to hear her recital, and then, too, there is always a special anxiety about performing for one's peers and for faculty members, as Robin would be doing in Paul Hall that Friday night.

Alan Weiss had just finished his lesson when we walked in. After Robin and Firkusny exchanged greetings, Alan and Robin discussed their schedules with Firkusny and agreed on when they would take their lessons the next day. In addition to preparing recitals, both were involved in end-of-semester exams. Firkusny said to Alan, "You need only an hour tomorrow. Everything is fine except the opening number—always the problem child." While Alan was packing up his music, he told Firkusny he had read a review in *High Fidelity* of Firkusny's recording of the Beethoven "Emperor" Concerto, with Uri Segal conducting the New Philharmonia. The critic Harris Goldsmith had liked the recording so much that he said he hoped Firkusny and Segal would record the four other Beethoven concertos. Firkusny smiled wryly. It was news to him that the record had been released. As a matter of fact, he hadn't even heard the lacquer—customarily sent to performers before the record is pressed. He seemed amused at a situation that might have prompted another artist to call his lawyer. Alan said before he left that he would bring Firkusny a copy of the review the next day.

Firkusny is a tall, lithe, trim man with gray hair, blue eyes, and smile lines in his face which soften an almost austere handsomeness. He was wearing a black turtleneck, gray slacks, and a gray jacket, and his manner was relaxed and friendly. His studio, on the fifth floor, has two Steinway grands side by side, a long, low gold couch against the wall behind the pianos, a gold rug, two green armchairs, and a large window with a view of Juilliard's interior marble courtyard and, on this day, a clear blue spring sky: a pocket of serenity at one of the busiest intersections in the city.

Robin seemed at ease, though there was a certain urgency in her manner. She had so little time—two days. "I'd like to start with the Chopin, if it's all right with you," she said. "I'm beginning to think of it as my nemesis."

Firkusny sat down on the couch and told her to begin.

Robin played all four movements without interruption, and almost before the last note had faded she spoke. "Am I taking the opening too fast? For some reason, I'm always scared of it."

"It's a difficult piece," Firkusny said.

"If I have trouble with it on this piano, heaven help me," Robin said. She then played the Ravel *Miroirs* straight through—"Noctuelles," "Oiseaux Tristes," "Une Barque sur l'Océan," "Alborada del Gracioso," and "La Vallée des Cloches."

When she had finished, Firkusny walked over to the other piano, sat down, and, referring to "Oiseaux Tristes," said, "Perhaps more concentration in the right hand." He played a high repeated figure—silken and articulated.

Robin said, "How do you get that balance?" and then, "Oh, it's the fingering. I was using five-four-three-two-one. You're using five-four-three-two-three."

"Don't change it now," Firkusny said. "But for the future . . . Do it slowly for me."

"Maybe I *can* change it now," Robin said. Firkusny moved over to her piano and, standing, played the figure on the lower part of the keyboard. Then they played it in unison several times, Robin in the upper register, trying the new fingering. "That *is* better," she said.

"But don't do it so—terribly *important*," Firkusny said. "You know?" He moved to the couch and hummed the theme as Robin played it again.

She played "Une Barque" and stopped at one point and tried a tremolo that melted from a double forte into a decrescendo. "I just can't lose enough sound," she said. "Should I release the pedal? Perhaps I'm not voicing this enough." As if to reassure him, she added, "Don't worry. I'm a fast worker. I still have time to change. Maybe I should bring the top out more. If I stop the trill earlier . . . Maybe if I stay piano longer . . ."

"It sounds fine," Firkusny said. "Don't worry so."

Nevertheless, Robin played "Une Barque" again, looking for a break or a division in a certain section. They agreed that there should be none. Firkusny said, "It should sound as one wash of color." He added, "Not because you should do it but because it interests me, why not try starting low and then gradually work into a crescendo—a big crescendo?"

Almost to herself, in exasperation, Robin said, "Why do

I keep breaking the line?" Then she played "Une Barque" through to the end.

Firkusny said, "This is charming."

Robin began the Schumann-Liszt lieder transcription, "Widmung," and for the first time Firkusny stopped her. He said, "Think of the voice. Always of the voice. He is singing to the girl he loves."

Robin laughed helplessly, and said, "*No* one could have sung it the way I did it. I was playing 'Mephisto.' How could I have missed the whole *character?*" She played it again, and he stood over her and softly hummed the melody, which was intertwined in a filigree of notes.

When she finished, he said, "The notes should be light, even though marked forte. A free sound—just the feeling of quiet ascending and descending chords."

She started again and played to the end, and he said, "Bravo! That's it. Very, very good."

Robin played "Hark, Hark, the Lark," a Schubert-Liszt transcription in which Liszt used repeated arpeggios containing the famous Schubert song. Firkusny told her not to emphasize the last note of the arpeggios so much, and then went to the other piano and played the arpeggio notes as chords, to demonstrate the effect he wanted.

"If I work, I can get it," Robin said. "Again, I missed the character." Then she quoted something that Mme. Dorfmann, who had been one of the C.A.G. judges, had said to her: "Don't try so *hard* the Chopin—let it come of itself as music that is in you." Robin added, "I still don't let it breathe in the right places. And I just can't seem to start the last movement without an accent."

Firkusny told her, "Why don't you start right in tempo? And the last movement is still a little tame."

"I know—it should cause chills," Robin said. "I'd like to keep it pianissimo, but then I lose tempo. I can't keep it going at the same presto speed."

"Basically, it's very good," he said. "I don't want to change it. I'm happy with the way you do it. It's yours, and it's convincing."

Robin told him that she had made a tape of Moussorgsky's *Pictures at an Exhibition* at radio station WNYC and that it would be broadcast the following Saturday morning, and that the studio piano had been shockingly bad. Firkusny said he was sorry that he wouldn't be able to hear it; he was going away. Robin said, "Well, I'm not sorry. I was so strung out from the competition I don't think I've ever played worse."

She returned to the Ravel and went over some of the problem spots. Of the "Noctuelles" she said, "I'm afraid I'm trying too many little things. It doesn't flow."

Firkusny said, "No, no. It is very good."

She picked up the score from the piano bench, flipped through the music, and pointed to a place on the page. "That's the spot. There are still some doubts."

She played it again, and he said, "That was beautiful, very beautiful."

Firkusny told Robin that after her lesson the next afternoon he would help her pick the piano she would use the night of her recital. (I pictured a sea of Steinways to choose from in Juilliard's basement, but later learned that the choice was between No. 1 and No. 3. No. 2, in the words of Josef Raieff, a concert pianist who teaches at the school, "died some time ago.") Robin said, "It won't take me long to choose. All I have to do is play this"—and she did fast repeated notes from "Alborada del Gracioso." Firkusny said that it was a little slow, and she laughed and said that it seemed fast to her.

She returned to the first movement of the Chopin. He stopped her and said, "If you rush the Grave, it loses in presence."

"I know, I know," she said, impatient with herself. She started again and played the complete movement. "Finally, I think I've got so I won't lose my head right on the first page."

"It's lovely—very, very lovely," Firkusny said.

Robin said, teasing, "You don't like my ending the program with the slow movement of the Ravel."

He said, "Yes, yes. It is all right."

She did the "Noctuelles" again, and he said, "Too fast—it's a bit rushed—and I don't hear enough right hand." He hummed the melody, inflecting a certain beat, which gave the theme the desired punctuation. It made sense to the ear.

Robin said, "That helps," and she played it again.

Firkusny smiled broadly and said, "That was nice. That's good. That's very, very good."

Robin asked, "Is the accelerando O.K.?"

He said, "It's fine. Let's go to the second one now."

She played "Oiseaux Tristes," and he said, "It sounds good, but start tranquillo."

She played "Une Barque" and said, "When I try for more volume, I lose the trill."

"Don't count the notes," Firkusny said. "Just play a tremolo." He came over and stood at the piano and played, to demonstrate. "Softer, and then nothing."

Robin said, "I think it's getting better—but then I heard the Lipatti recording."

She played "Alborada del Gracioso," and when she had

finished he said, "The accents could be better. Not louder but sharper—a more intense quality but not more volume." She repeated a passage—one note struck repeatedly, rapidly, twelve times—and he said, "It's good. It could be better. Here you are still a little bit nervous. You are rushing it, and therefore you can't play all twelve notes clearly. It should be like one note. What is important is the first note and the last. It is like a guitar—it is blocked, you know." She played the entire piece again, and now he said, "Bravo! Bravo!"

She said, "Is the recitative O.K.? It seems to get slower. And I think I try to play too pianissimo."

"It should be." He sat at the other piano and played the passage, exaggerating the rhythm. They both laughed. "It must be rough, offensive," he said of a passage Robin felt was not loud enough. "But to force is ruinous."

Robin said, "I start with the fourth finger. Maybe I should change that."

He said, "It's color you need." He flipped through the score, pointing to different passages and saying, "Excellent . . . Good . . . Perfect . . ." Of one passage, he said, "You must keep it *mercilessly* in rhythm." She played the passage while he stood and beat time on the piano.

They discussed possible English titles for the Ravel pieces and agreed that in some cases there were no accurate translations. One, Firkusny said, might suggest moths or fireflies, but only in marshes, and one the morning song of a medieval jester. He asked what the English term was for a small fishing boat. Robin said she thought it was "small cruiser," and he laughed and said, "Not on the program, I hope."

It had been a long lesson, and it was time to go. Robin

gathered her music together and told Firkusny she would play her encores for him the following day.

On the night of Robin's recital, Paul Hall was almost full by eight o'clock. Robin's mother, who had arrived in town the night before, was in the audience, as was Richard Campbell, a friend of Robin's from Seattle, who had brought with him on the plane a twenty-two-pound salmon for a post-recital reception in Jane Harris's apartment. Firkusny, his wife, and Mme. Dorfmann were in the audience, and several other faculty members were there—a good sign. I spotted Robin peering through a small window at the left of the stage which provided a view of the auditorium, and shortly after eight, when everyone was seated and the lights had been dimmed, she came onstage. She was wearing a floor-length lime-green chiffon dress with long, full sleeves and a full skirt, which moved gracefully as she walked to the piano. She acknowledged the applause with a smile and a nod, and, seated at the piano, remained motionless for a moment, hands in lap, eyes downcast. (Robin had told me once that she no longer suffered from acute stagefright—and that she was happy because, with rare exceptions, she could channel the inevitable adrenalin flow into her music. She hastened to add that of course she was nervous—only a child or an idiot wouldn't be—but that the feeling now was one of delicious dread, a mixture of horror and anticipation.)

Her playing that night had a special excitement. There were no problems in the Chopin, and the last movement, which she took at an exhilarating speed, did indeed cause chills, as she had said it should. The Ravel had an ethereal beauty, and at times, because of the delicacy of her playing

—the subtle, whispering pianissimos—the piano ceased to sound like a percussion instrument.

When it was all over, she came out repeatedly to acknowledge the applause. Richard Fields climbed the steps to the stage, presented her with several bouquets of flowers, and kissed her on the cheek. Robin plucked a flower from one of the bouquets, handed it to him, and returned the kiss. Then she placed the flowers on the floor in front of the piano, sat down, and played the Liszt "Gnomenreigen" Étude. She looked radiant during the final bows—particularly beautiful and relaxed now that it was over, and apparently pleased with how it had gone.

Robin, as is the custom, waited in the Green Room to accept compliments and talk with the people who came backstage, and by the time she arrived at the reception, Jane's living room was filled with friends, relatives, teachers, and fellow-students. Everyone applauded, and there were shouts of "Bravo!" She stood on the balcony and smiled and waved and said, "Thank you, thank you. You can pick up your checks on the way out."

A bar had been set up in the dining room, and a long antique refectory table held—in addition to the salmon, which had been poached in Jane's kitchen that afternoon—an assortment of hot and cold dishes, all provided by Robin's friends for the occasion. Roman Markowicz, Alan Weiss, and Richard Fields talked to Robin about the program and commented on things that they thought she had done especially well. Alan complimented her on her enviable finesse. Robin said the piano was terrible—almost a P.S.O., or piano-shaped object.

Josef Raieff was standing nearby, and I asked him why Juilliard couldn't provide a better piano for its recital hall.

He said, "Those pianos are subject to extraordinary wear and tear, and we do our best to keep them in tune and in good repair, but it's a losing battle. Our piano technician, Matthias Barth, is one of the best, but when you realize that a piano is often tuned every twenty minutes during a recording session, maybe you can understand the insurmountable task of even keeping abreast of—not to mention ahead of—over two hundred pianos and two hundred students. A piano might look indestructible, but it's a delicate instrument." He watched the young pianists talking animatedly, and he smiled. He said, "Actually, they're a little naïve. When they get out in the world, they're going to look back rather fondly at Juilliard's pianos."

Robin's mother, in a sisterly, almost identical green dress, accepted congratulations from the guests Jane introduced to her. Mrs. McCabe is a youthful-looking woman, and a stranger could have identified her as Robin's mother, the resemblance is so marked. She came with me into a den off the dining room to tell me something about Robin's early life.

"Robin learned fast," Mrs. McCabe said, "too fast, actually. Her playing was not always accurate, and in the beginning we had to weed out the McCabe notes from the Mozart. When she was almost five, I took her to a women's-club luncheon, and she played a little piece for the ladies. I think it was something called 'Spooky Hollow.' I remember she was wearing a cute little red dress and black patent-leather Mary Janes, and she looked very serious while she played. When she'd finished, she ran to me and buried her face in my lap." She paused and smiled at the memory. "During the drive home, she asked me, 'When can I be on the menu?'"

Many parents have trouble getting their children to practice; often, lessons are provided not to produce a prodigy but to enrich the child's life, but sometimes the more it means to the parents, it seems, the more the child resists. Part of the explanation is undoubtedly that the child is asked to learn the tiresome techniques of playing long before he can anticipate the beauty of music. But Mrs. McCabe said, "Getting Robin to practice was never a problem. I think it can be a lonely thing to do, even boring, in the early stages. The scales and exercises aren't much fun, though they are *so* important. I think the fact that I sat with her while she worked probably helped. She always had a special fondness for music—she loved it from the beginning. There's also a bit of the ham in Robin. She likes to play for people, and that was a big help when she started giving recitals and entering competitions."

Robin's emotional equilibrium before a competition or a performance is unusual, and I asked Mrs. McCabe if her daughter had always been like that.

She said, "Robin has certainly had her share of butterflies. The times she did get nervous about playing, she would let it all out verbally—become vociferous, almost belligerent. Once, I was driving her to a competition—I think she was thirteen or fourteen—and she was whining and complaining. She'd had a bad lesson, she didn't like one of the pieces she was going to play, I think she'd heard that another girl would be at the contest who would be hard to beat. It's so long ago . . . Anyway, she complained so much that I stopped the car and said, 'Tell me what you want to do. If all this is just subterfuge to shake me up so I feel as bad as you do, then we'll go on. But if you really feel that bad, let's go home.' I think she realized then that she shouldn't be thinking just of herself, and after that she was more considerate, more mature."

Young musicians who are pushed hard in the beginning and have few outlets in other activities often have emotional problems later in life. Mrs. McCabe said that Robin had always had other interests. In her early teens, she would rather watch a ballgame than hear someone else perform; in fact, she played the glockenspiel in the high-school band, so she could see all the games. "She loves to ski, and is very good at it, and she is an exceptionally fine tennis player," Mrs. McCabe said. "She was asked to be on the high-school team, but the muscles involved in playing tennis can strain those used playing the piano. She was disappointed that she had to refuse, but we tried to make it up to her—with more skiing, and trips to Sun Valley, and weekends at our cottage in Idaho. Also, Robin's friends often came over to swim in our pool. She gets very involved in everything she does—applies to it the same intensity and concentration she applies to music."

Mrs. McCabe told me that someone had asked her recently what she thought her most important contribution to Robin's musical development was, and she had said, "Picking up the pieces after a disappointment—a second instead of a first in a competition." She said that it was never hard for Robin to accept losing if she felt she hadn't played well but that when she knew she had, and didn't win, she felt crushed. "Logically, when you're in many competitions in the same area, the blessings have to be passed around," Mrs. McCabe said. "It's not possible to win every contest. We had clichés for such times: 'It's the law of averages,' 'You've got to learn to accept losing,' 'It's part of life,' 'The best performers don't necessarily win all the time.' "

Mrs. McCabe said that Robin's two sisters were still taking piano lessons. Rachelle, who was eighteen, was very serious about it, but Renée, who was twelve, said she would rather be a stewardess. "I tell Renée she can't quit—she has to keep going, or she won't have anything to talk about with her sisters."

Robin called to her mother from the doorway to come and meet the Firkusnys and Mme. Dorfmann, and we both returned to the dining room. The crowd had thinned out somewhat, the din of voices diminished. Mitchell Andrews was standing in the archway between the dining room and the living room, and I went over to talk with him. He has had a successful, varied career as a soloist, a chamber-music player, and an accompanist. Andrews told me now that he thought Robin's recital had gone well. He said, "I like her playing very much. She seems so calm and collected, with no stiffness or posing—almost regal, extremely well under control. That, to me, is one of the exciting things about her. We don't see any emotion to speak of and everything sounds so beautiful, and all of a sudden she lashes out in a big climax and then she moves somewhat. It all seems to arise from some inner core of excitement that was there the whole time, and you realize it's not an inconsistency in her playing when these big moments come. I like playing that doesn't go in for a lot of movement at the piano. The less body English you use, the better you play the instrument. Also, she's very positive in her approach: she starts when she's ready, and not before."

Robin had moved to Jane's Steinway, at the far end of the

living room, kicked off her silver sandals, and begun to play. A piano is a magnet to her, and now that most of the guests had left, and nothing remained of the salmon but the skeleton, she was enjoying playing another kind of music —Cole Porter. Richard Fields, Richard Campbell, Richard Fredrickson, a bass player with whom Robin had taped a recital for educational television, Alan, and Roman gathered round. Robin switched from Porter to a game she likes to play. She began a Beethoven sonata and after the first phrase suddenly segued into a Bartók in the same key, and in this manner she switched from one composer to another —Liszt, Falla, Mozart, Prokofieff, Scriabin—until everyone was laughing. A guessing game followed, with the young musicians taking turns trying to outwit one another. The idea was to play the first chord of a piano composition and see if the others could name it. Roman was especially quick, and was not stumped even when Robin played a single note; he said, "The 'Appassionata.' " Then Richard Fields held both hands in chord position in midair and Roman named the correct Liszt piece. Richard Fredrickson played a chord that baffled all the others, and when he said it was the "Trout" Quintet they called him a cheat—chamber music was not supposed to be included. Only Alan Weiss stumped them. He played a chord and waited, and finally told them it was "Nach Bach"—a modern work. When I left, at one in the morning, Roman and Richard Fields were playing Mozart duets.

Chapter

5

On May 25th, Robin had her first post-recital lesson with Firkusny. Before they got down to serious work, she said she wanted to do something special for him. She played "Satin Doll," and told him it was in honor of Duke Ellington, who had died the day before.

When Robin comes onstage to play, she often sits a minute, hands in lap, profile to the audience. The result is that the audience seems to be invited into the music just as she is tuning the audience out. I commented on this to Robin. It was the week following her recital, and we were having lunch in the Juilliard cafeteria.

"There are some pieces—bravura pieces—that you can plunge right into, and that can be very effective," she said. "Others require self-containment, a feeling within yourself that I think of as a vibration. You have to allow this to come out. More and more, I've become aware of something that's exhilarating and at the same time disconcerting—that in performance sometimes the greatest things happen almost in spite of you. It's a little frightening and a little maddening. But it's still exhilarating, because it signifies total freedom. All the mechanics are there, the rudiments. You're basically drilled, the muscle memory is there, and something inside you says, 'All right, let's see what happens. Let this happen.' I had that experience in the 'Funeral March' movement a couple of times the other night. I knew that it was going well, and a voice inside me said, 'Try this.' When that happens, you're above the practice-room experience. It's a wonderful feeling. I think it was Stravinsky who said, 'Your freedom comes from your discipline.' "

Before the recital, Robin had seemed particularly concerned about the Chopin and the Beethoven, and I asked if they were both new to her.

"Only the Chopin, though the Beethoven is still slightly green," she said. "The Beethoven bothered me because it was the first piece on the program and is a difficult one to start out with. The first movement is extremely treacherous. Most pianists let the tempo run away. I knew the things I wanted to happen, and they couldn't if I let my nerves get the better of me. The Chopin was new, and it's an unusual piece. It doesn't suit the piano, fit the hand, the way most Chopin works do. It's new, and in some sections the freedom isn't there. And again, I was afraid of nerves. I was still thinking of what was the right thing to do instead of what was the thing that wanted to come out of me. I remember what Satie said about his own compositions—how he worked. He said, 'I always like to walk around a piece several times, accompanied by myself.' And Charles Ives said that you should never play a piece the same way twice. He compared it to viewing a piece of sculpture from different angles. It all takes time. Next year, I'll play the Beethoven differently. In twenty years, the Chopin won't be the same. I have a tremendous respect for the Chopin. You take your life in your hands when you play it. It's so well known—it's included in so many recitals. There has to be individuality. You can't copy anybody. It has to come from the heart, and that takes time. Some pianists try to emulate the so-called Chopin style—which seems meaningless to me. We don't know how he played. We know what he was like as a person. It's the same thing when we try to resolve the controversy about playing Bach. His music was written for the harpsichord, the clavichord, or the organ. Should we, then, try to produce a small sound, an intimate sound? Should we try to terrace our dynamics the way they did on the harpsichord? It seems to me these things can only be worked out by individual judgment."

That week, Robin had gone to Town Hall for the New York début recital of another Juilliard pupil—a young man from Sweden named Marian Migdal. Donal Henahan had covered it for the *Times,* and though he conceded that Migdal had technique—almost too much; he called him "finger-proud"—the pianist otherwise left him cold. Robin said she agreed with the review. "He lacked nuance, color. The Chopin was much too fast. I'd heard him before, and I don't think he was at his best that night. He's a beautiful pianist. I'm sure Mme. Dorfmann is furious with the review, because he's her star pupil. I played the Chopin for him before the contest, and he gave me some valuable help. He's recorded it in Europe. But the night of his début he played it matter-of-factly. And Henahan's phrase 'finger-proud'— I've never heard it before. It's a perceptive statement. You have to be careful. You have all this machinery, and if you let it go with nothing behind it—no emotional channeling —the audience gets the feeling 'So what?' Fortunately, one review won't wipe him out of the ballgame. Unfortunately, there's not much he can extract from it." (Migdal was apparently not damaged by the review; he is now playing in Europe, and his career is flourishing.)

Henahan's review led Robin to talk about other kinds of criticism. In the past, she told me, she had encountered one teacher who had a reputation for being cruel to his pupils. "There are so many ways of criticizing without devastating a person," she said. "I was in one of his master classes, and he told one young boy, very sarcastically, 'We count the flies on the ceiling while you play.' It was funny, and we all laughed, but it was cruel. Perhaps one needs a strong ego to take any kind of criticism in this field. Perhaps the teacher was trying to tell the kid that he doesn't have what it takes for a career. If so, he should have told him directly. I think this is especially true for a boy. A girl—well, it's a cliché that she doesn't have to have a career. But a boy— if he's committing himself totally to this and he doesn't have the stamina and endurance and consistency, not to mention the talent, he should be *told* before he has wasted half his life and set himself up for crushing disappointment."

Migdal's début had drawn a small audience, Robin said, and Town Hall had looked depressingly empty. She said that one reason she had entered the Concert Artists Guild competition was that she wanted to make her début in Carnegie Recital Hall—the smallest auditorium in New York that is covered by *Times* critics. She reasoned that she could possibly fill the hall and thus insure more excitement. Most débuts attract very few people aside from relatives and friends. She had considered entering the Naumburg, but if she had won that, her début would have been in Alice Tully Hall. Besides, the repertoire requirements included a big American piece. She played the Copland Sonata, but she didn't consider it a good piece for her—she said she tends to fall in love with pieces she really likes and really works on. "I don't play it well yet," she said of the Copland, and she went on, "If I'm still in this game in a year or two, I'll try for the Leventritt. That's an enormous competition." She said that no one had advised her to enter the Concert Artists Guild competition—Firkusny had been on tour when she made the decision—and she added, "I really didn't expect to win, I really had no hopes. I'm a born pessimist when it comes to things like that. I suppose it's a safety valve to keep me from being too disappointed. I tell myself, 'Always expect the worst, and you'll never be disappointed.' I guess deep down I don't believe it. I have a theory that in the music business moderato will get you no place."

Of contests in general and the difficulties of being interrupted erratically by the judges, Robin said, "Playing in such circumstances doesn't leave you with a very good feeling. You try not to anticipate the interruption. If you think about it, you're not creating very much. You can't play to a jury—you've got to immerse yourself in the music. My teacher Béla Siki has judged the Leeds Competition, in England, several times. That's a beautiful competition—a huge competition. Wonderful prizes. You get a guaranteed broadcast with the BBC and lots of concerts. Siki says that when you're on a jury, listening all day, you know in a few minutes whether you need to listen further. No matter what the contestant is playing, it's got to be something that comes across right away. I asked him, 'What if it starts really badly?' and he said, 'Well, you try not to close your ears. Give it a little more chance.'

"If you're not doing well, in the back of your mind you know it. But you try not to think of that. You try to redeem yourself somewhere, somehow. I played in a competition in Washington and made a bad stumble in the cadenza of the Beethoven Third Concerto. It sounded really bad. But I told myself, 'Now you've got to do something good.' And it got better. I thought afterward that I'd done some gross things for a few seconds, and that maybe I was finished, but I won. It takes discipline, and you learn it or else. The conductor Michael Tilson Thomas has an apt saying: 'Applaud thyself not. C sharp and B natural.' Another thing he says is 'Talent plus chutzpah equals bravo.' And I think it's true. If you lack the drive and the nerve to push yourself even when you have misgivings over what you're about to attempt, not many people are going to push you. The world's too busy and moving too fast. But you must not take whatever happens—especially adversity—personally. You develop a thicker skin as you go along. I know that my playing right now doesn't reach certain people, that there are things they disapprove of. But you have to decide for yourself that there's some good there anyway."

After a brief pause, Robin went on, "It's getting harder, though. I'm convinced that fifty years ago a pianist could get by with pyrotechnics, histrionics, and lots of flair. But audiences are better educated now. Recordings have done it. In a way, it's sad. We go out with an image of Richter playing the 'Appassionata' and it's hard not to think, My God, why even try? You have to forget that. I think that the moment you walk out onstage, and not before—in that moment you have to decide that there's something special about the way you play the piece that is different from anyone else's. There's something unique, and you deserve this moment to be heard. But if you think, Oh, compared to So-and-So this sounds terrible, you might as well forget it."

I asked Robin who some of her heroes were, and she said, "When I was very young, Cliburn. I'd read and heard so much about him. I still think he's great, though it's become chic to put him down. He received so much publicity as the blond Apollo who broke through the Iron Curtain. Now he's getting flogged by the press because he hasn't expanded his repertoire—he tends to play the same program. He takes it in stride and with good humor. He told me, 'I talked to Ashkenazy, and he teased me about playing the same piece all the time. So I said to him, "Vladie, I will play the perfect program. I'll start with the Sonata in F Minor —Beethoven. Next piece—Sonata Opus 57—Beethoven. Intermission. Sonata 'Appassionata'—Beethoven."' He plays that piece all the time, but it's not totally his fault— he does so many concerts a year and when he appears with an orchestra, people don't want to hear the Ravel Concerto. They want to hear the Rachmaninoff, the Tchaikovsky." She paused. "Well, maybe he should slow down." She went on to say that everyone found him likable. "He has terrific family loyalty. He can talk Wall Street, books, politics. He loves life. The fact that he's outgoing has been a big asset. And he is a *great* talent—there's no doubt about it. He has a very special, luscious tone. He's become highly popular with audiences but scorned by critics. He's now the blue-collar pianist. It seems unfair to put him down." After a minute, she added, "It's no longer easy to list the top greats in the piano world. There are so many."

I wondered if the crowded field made her feel threatened, and she said, "Actually, it's almost comforting. There's a certain salvation in being in a sea of anonymity. Also, in spite of the tremendous numbers, everybody has his favorites. This is the age of individuality—you can do different things and be appreciated for them. I couldn't begin to name my favorites. I go through periods when I'm a Horowitz freak. Rubinstein seems to transcend the whole performance idea of the moment onstage. He's lived such a marvelous life that we all have to look at it and learn from him. Any man who can give so much to the public . . . There's something very pure-spirited about him. Perhaps it goes with greatness. I do think his recordings are on a lower level than his live performances. Someone suggested that if he invited just five people into the recording studio to play to, the recordings would be better. Rubinstein makes the legend about himself, because of his antics and his public life. Horowitz is the opposite. He does nothing, but the legend continues. You hear little about Horowitz the man. But there's such an aura, a mystique about him.

Many pianists try to imitate him. Everybody has tried to copy what he does in the 'Funeral March' of the Chopin—the part after the trio, the very beautiful theme in the major key. It's marked piano in the score. Horowitz brings it back forte. I've tried it, and it doesn't work. It has to come from him."

Robin quoted a cliché in the music world—"There's nothing as dead as yesterday's performance"—and commented, "I prefer not to believe it. It might be true if you compare a performance with a painting—the performance is no longer 'in the air.' But there is gratification for the listener as well as the performer in remembering how certain things went.

"Stanislavski equated life in the theatre with running the gauntlet. That is true of music, too. It can be a terrible business trying to exert your own personality and be a creative artist. He said a very important thing of young people: 'You have to like the art in you, not yourself in the art.' That says so much. I know so many people who are in love with the *idea* of themselves as artists or musicians, and it gives them an identity, an illusion, and if they discover they really can't deliver they often go off the deep end. But if you can see yourself as having something that is worth developing, that deserves reverence and regard, and it is an art you know, then it sees you through the bad times. In a way, it's like looking at yourself as an enzyme, more than anything else. You're an enzyme, and you hope the catalysts are right, so you come out with something really good. The interpreter's role is a tremendously responsible one. You're given a great work of art—a Beethoven sonata, say —and what do you do with it? First of all, you try to be faithful to the score, try to give allegiance to it. But there has to be something of you in the performance, in your rendition or reading of it, that is unique and reflects your insights. Part of it is possibly self-containment. You have to like yourself. You can't function well if you're basically insecure about what's inside you. And if music is only a medium for asserting your ego, then you're in trouble. The life of a musician is a rarefied one. If you know there's something inside you, and you're respectful of it, and you know that your job is to develop it and have others help you develop it, then you're going to do something. You might develop something that's different. Maybe not better than what anyone else has done, but something worth working on. Such thoughts help me and sustain me."

Robin said that she usually enjoys practicing, but added, "Some days, I look at that keyboard and it looks like a giant leering mouth with hundreds of sharp teeth. I swear, I can't even see a piano. I see this box with all these teeth, glaring at me. And I think, I don't want to go *near* you today. Sometimes it's a mood of the day, or it arises from something that happened to me beforehand—some disillusionment. It might not even be related to music. Or it can happen after a bad lesson. I usually force myself to practice then. If that's too painful, I write in a notebook. If I've had a really rotten lesson, I don't want to think about it. But I force myself to do that, too. I'll write a sentence the teacher said, an adjective he used, and I'll underline it, and sometimes poke holes in the page because I'm so mad at myself."

A bad lesson, Robin said, was one in which she had been shortsighted—had failed in a proper interpretation of a piece—or had played something she had worked on a great deal and felt proud of, and discovered "how *green* it still is." She said, "There are certain times when I've studied a piece and either I haven't taken the time or I've gone about it in a careless way, and it shows. My teacher can just zero in on one phrase, and it's immediately obvious that what I've done is so immature it makes me feel like an absolute schlepp."

She turned to the subject of her taste in music, saying, "Sometimes I have a certain feeling about a piece—an inner conviction that I will play it well. Other times, I have what amounts to a hunch about a piece—that I'd really rather not play it at this point in my life. At the moment, I don't feel much affinity with contemporary composers, though I like their music when it's played well. At one stage, I didn't even like playing Bach, which seems unbelievable now. I'm beginning to love some of the small Beethoven pieces, and the Schubert-Liszt transcriptions I did in my recital. Three years ago, I didn't know they existed. Like many young pianists, I came to Juilliard armed with big, bravura pieces, but I've relaxed somewhat, and no longer feel the urge to be histrionic. I find myself thinking in more intimate terms. I'm paying more attention to vocal literature—learning to listen to arias, songs. It helps with what is in fact a percussion instrument to become more aware of melodic lines. When I spoke of 'voicing' in my lesson, I meant bringing out an inner voice that needs some emphasis to be heard at all. Glenn Gould—whom I consider rather an eccentric pianist—is famous for bringing out inner voices. Chopin is thought of primarily as a melodic composer, but that seems inaccurate to me. There's beautiful counterpoint in his compositions that isn't brought out very often in performance. In some pieces, he uses the piano like a toy —flashing scales, arpeggios. The sonata I did in my recital is not as pianistic as most of his works. That eerie last movement . . . It's been nicknamed 'The Wind over the Grave.' Starting it is like jumping off a cliff. There's no looking back. There's a temptation to take a safe tempo, but it would be ruinous. I find myself thinking every time I start it, Please, God, let it come."

Robin laughed at herself, and said, "If you mistrust yourself when you're playing that fast, if the brain suddenly says, 'Here comes the spot where I might have trouble,' then you've had it. Béla Siki says, 'In the moment of performance, you have to *trust* yourself. You ask no questions.' When you're practicing, you question everything—every phrase. Ask how should it be constructed, where is it going, where is the top point. But in the moment of performance you can't think of any of these things. I've heard pianists have memory slips, and I could hear the slip coming. I can hear when something becomes tentative. You can almost tell when muscle memory is taking over. Perhaps the pianist is questioning something, or he's thinking of someone in the audience. And then the slip will happen. The concentration must be the most demanding of anything anyone does in this world: the things you have to remember, the things you must tune out of your mind—whispering ladies, cellophane wrappers, flapping programs, creaking piano stools."

Robin said that she had been working so hard recently that she had had little time left for fun, but she added, "I have some good friends—a couple of boyfriends who are very nice, very understanding. I'm somewhat of a loner at this point in my life. I haven't met anyone who's managed to interfere with this drive. I shouldn't say 'interfere,' because when it happens it will be very nice. But it will take a strong personality. I think I'm rather hard on the boys I go out with, because there is this conflict—I don't have the *time* to be involved. Sooner or later, they get the impression that they're playing second fiddle to a Steinway, and it must be hard to take. Also, in addition to practicing six or seven hours a day—twelve, if I'm really working—I have a great need for privacy. I need time to answer mail, do bookwork. Some nights, I pray there won't be any telephone messages for me, because I'll have to answer them."

Robin has the reputation at Juilliard of being a hard worker; in 1973, Juilliard awarded her the Albert Szirmai Scholarship and in 1974 the Ruth D. Rosenman Scholarship—both for outstanding achievement in piano. She felt that she had inched her way up to the middle-gun level, and the other students seemed nicer. "Probably because I've become friendlier," she said. "Also, I try not to interfere in any practice-room intrigues—and there are a million of them going on. There's quite a bit of gossip, back-stabbing. It can take up your whole life if you let it. Some kids seem to like to kvetch at great length. What's the use?" Robin seldom eats in the Juilliard cafeteria, because the temptation to linger over coffee and talk is too great. The gossip at Juilliard is usually about who is having an affair with whom, or which marriage has just broken up—often because one career is doing better than another.

I had an idea that the lesson I had heard with Firkusny was not typical of the way he taught, since it was just before her recital, and teachers tend to be reluctant to try many changes at such a late date, but Robin said that in a way it had been, though his letting her play the Chopin and the Ravel without interruption was—with the recital so close —unusual and valuable. "He likes to polish fine points. He takes it for granted that when I bring a piece to him it will be at an advanced stage—that I will have worked on it a long time myself. He got down to brass tacks in that lesson —especially in the Ravel."

Mention of Robin's recital reminded her of one that she had given in Puyallup the previous summer. "There was an American flag onstage, with a spotlight trained on it, and I started with 'The Star-Spangled Banner'—a huge arrangement, à la Cliburn," she told me. "I did it for several psychological reasons. I wanted to put the audience at ease. About a thousand people had bought tickets, many of whom probably hadn't been to a recital before. They came because my father was their doctor—small-town people who might be put off by Bach, Debussy, Falla, Beethoven. I also did it to please myself. I guess I'm old-fashioned, but it made me feel good. It was quite dramatic. Those who knew me probably thought, She's been in New York for two years, and she hasn't changed a bit. For encores, I did my own arrangement of Gershwin's 'The Man I Love,' and then Streisand's 'Happy Days Are Here Again.' It's a great piece—that arrangement. Very slow, lots of pathos. The chords are *so* good. I copied it from the record shamelessly. It brought down the house. It was really fun to do, though I would never do that kind of thing in New York. I didn't mean to play down to them. But it's very important to gauge your audience's tolerance level—decide what it's receptive to, what it can take, warm it up. I feel that performing is show business to a certain extent. You can't play only to musicians."

The cafeteria had emptied while we talked, and was about to close. Robin said she had a million things to do before she left town for the summer. She had found a small apartment in the West Seventies and wanted to get at least

[73]

partly moved. Also, her sister Rachelle was giving a recital at the University of Washington the following weekend, and Robin didn't want to miss it. As we were leaving the building, we met Roman. He had given his recital the night before. With practically no advance notice, he had been given a hall to play in—the Juilliard Theatre—and even so he had had a good-sized audience, which included Robin. Roman said he was exhausted from the recital; the piano's action was so stiff he was worn out. (The Juilliard Theatre piano is one of the very few pianos in the school that aren't given a daily, steady workout.) Then Roman asked Robin if she had liked his Bach, and she said she had, very much, and congratulated him on his large audience. Not many students could almost fill the theatre, she said. Roman said, "With a Polish family, that's one thing you can count on." He told Robin that Mme. Dorfmann had been so angry with him that she hadn't come backstage afterward to congratulate him. Robin, who had already heard this—news travels fast at Juilliard—asked why, and Roman said, "I didn't play the way *she* wanted me to play. I played the way *I* wanted to. I am not a Coca-Cola—a crowd pleaser."

Chapter

6

Robin spent the first part of the summer of 1974—
after a week of tennis and swimming and no practicing
—teaching at the University of Washington and taking
lessons from Béla Siki. In August, she went as a student
to the Shawnigan Summer School of the Arts, on Van-
couver Island. The school's faculty consists of performing artists, who coach students and give chamber-music
concerts three times a week. The session lasted four
weeks, and at the end of it Robin was asked to return

the following summer as a member of the faculty.

In the fall, Robin settled into her small apartment—"barely big enough to turn around in"—and, having been granted a teaching fellowship at Juilliard, began teaching there. She did a number of programs in the New York area—some arranged by the Concert Artists Guild and some as a result of invitations from various schools and institutions that had heard about her—and, with her New York début looming on April 1st, 1975, she practiced every minute she could. She spent Christmas with her family, in Puyallup, and, back in New York, in February, she began studying with Mme. Dorfmann. In March, she did a run-through of her recital program at Jane's for some fellow-students, including Richard Fields, Alan, and Roman. She wanted to see where the weak spots were—where she might still be a bit insecure. She had decided to do the Chopin and two pieces from *Miroirs*. She would start with the Beethoven Andante Favori, followed by the Chopin, and then the Scriabin Sonata No. 4 in F Sharp Major, Opus 30. After the intermission, she would play the Sonatine for left hand by Dinu Lipatti, "Une Barque" and "Alborada del Gracioso," and the "Mephisto Waltz" No. 1 of Liszt. After Robin had played through her program and listened to her friends' comments, she returned to the "Funeral March," but after the first, somber eight bars she suddenly segued into a lilting "Smoke Gets in Your Eyes" in the major key. Everyone laughed—Roman dared her to do it at her recital—and the intense scene dissolved into a party.

Robin's mother and father both came to New York to hear her début, and so did Richard Campbell, who was now the music-and-art critic of the Seattle *Post-Intelligencer*. On the night of the recital, Robin's father took her down to the

Recital Hall. He said later that he had never seen her so apprehensive or nervous. She asked to be driven around the block three times before she finally went in. It was a very serious, solemn Robin who came onstage at eight-thirty. She was wearing a vibrant-pink dress, similar in cut to the full-sleeved green one (for freedom and comfort). She had filled the hall, as she had hoped she would, and everything went well. During the intermission, her mother tried, without success, to get backstage. She thought Robin looked very pale, and wanted her to put on more lipstick. There is a special vulnerability about someone making a New York début, and when Robin's was over she received thunderous applause and shouts of "Bravo!" from her friends, partly as a way of patting her on the back reassuringly.

At a reception in the apartment of Harry Kreindler, a friend who lives on Central Park West, Robin still seemed tense, and, with the exception of a beaming Dr. McCabe, the party seemed almost funereal. Though Robin was pleased with the way she had played, who knew what the *Times* critic would say? In the back of her mind was a bad review Alan Weiss had got three months earlier, when he made his début. The critic had complained that Alan had practiced too much—that there was no spontaneity in his playing, and that it was annoyingly perfect. Alan was considered one of the best pianists at Juilliard, and everyone from the school felt that he had played beautifully; no one could understand the harsh review. Robin didn't know who had covered her recital for the *Times*. (Sometimes, for a number of reasons—the tickets don't arrive at the *Times* or the performance is so bad that silence is charity—no review appears, and every performer fears, first, no review and, second, a bad one.) Some of her friends hoped that it had not been Donal Henahan, who, even when he likes a performer, can inject a barb or cast a doubt. ("If his recital yesterday afternoon at Alice Tully Hall was not merely one of those freakishly great days that good pianists sometimes enjoy, Seymour Bernstein is ready to break out into a wider circle of attention.") Robin said that if she had appeared grim while she was playing, it was because the piano was so bad; she had had trouble adjusting to it, to make the most of what it had to offer. Bloch was at the reception, and I asked him why Robin—or any pianist, for that matter— didn't rent a good piano for such an important occasion. He said that the backstage area of the Recital Hall was too small to hold an extra nine-foot grand, and no one wanted to do a recital on a smaller piano.

The *Times* has a policy of printing most reviews of week-night débuts in the Sunday edition, and Robin had to wait five days to read hers. Raymond Ericson was the critic, and the review was good:

> Robin McCabe, who made her local début under the auspices of the Concert Artists Guild in Carnegie Recital Hall last Tuesday night, is a talented and independent-minded young pianist. A West Coast artist, she has recently been studying at the Juilliard School with Rudolf Firkusny and Ania Dorfmann.
>
> In Chopin's "Funeral March" Sonata, she asserted her musical personality with a number of interesting details, rubatos, stressing of inner voices, unusual dynamics. She had a marked ability to use varying tonal attacks provocatively, and this came to the fore in Scriabin's Sonata No. Four in F Sharp. She gave this a lightly febrile, almost skittish performance. It was less intense and emotionally possessed than normal, but it was no less effective because of its pointillist coloration.
>
> The snapping rhythms of Ravel's "Alborada del Graci-

oso" were equally striking in Miss McCabe's performance, and she gave a full-blooded version of Liszt's "Mephisto Waltz" No. 1.

A novelty of sorts was Dinu Lipatti's Sonatine for the
left hand alone. Written in 1947, it is an attractive piece,
but like most of its kind, more interesting in its clever use
of one hand than for the music itself. It was an excellent
vehicle for the pianist, whose technically adroit left hand
was put to good use in the more conventional works, too.

Still, one review was not enough to get a managing agent
interested in her, and such interest—which was often
aroused after a pianist won a major competition or two—
would offer her about the only hope for a career.

Firkusny arranged a meeting between Robin and Andre
Kostelanetz. If Kostelanetz liked her playing, perhaps he
would use her in one of the New York Philharmonic Promenade Concerts he conducts in the spring. Several months
later, Robin played for him at his apartment. He liked her
playing—told her that she played beautifully and could
obviously play anything, and that he would keep her in
mind. Robin said later that he had made no promises but
had given her some advice. He told her, "You have to keep
beating your head against the wall until you come to a soft
spot, and then you must beat even harder."

One night in early June, after Juilliard had closed for the
day, I spoke with Robin again. She had been hard at work
practicing for a three-week South American tour, and she
was leaving the next morning. I asked how the tour had
been arranged, and she said, "The State Department asked
the Dean, Gideon Waldrop, to recommend someone the
school thought would be a good representative, and my
name was one of the ones he suggested. I was asked to send

[79]

my dossier—my propaganda—to Washington, and they were apparently satisfied, because I was chosen."

I had been curious for some time about what motivates young artists—what keeps the Robins and the Alans and the others going—and I asked her now. "If you love music, performing is, of course, more gratifying than listening," Robin replied. "You can multiply almost to infinity the pleasure of listening in order to gauge the immense satisfaction of playing. Obviously, it is essential to have a performing temperament. You actually live for those moments of being onstage. I have a tremendous desire to perform, and that keeps me going. When you perform, you become the protagonist. And if you don't have the outlet of performing it can be terribly frustrating. I guess the truth is that I feel most attractive, most complete as a person when I'm playing for an audience."

In recent years, a number of pianists have chosen to specialize in certain composers—Lili Kraus in Mozart, Ruth Laredo in Scriabin and Rachmaninoff, William Masselos in modern works, Grant Johannesen in French composers—and I asked Robin which composers she liked at this point. "Of course, nobody can be all things to all styles of music," she said. "Right now, I definitely feel more comfortable in anything but the classic style. The Baroque style, yes. The Romantic, the French Impressionists, I feel especially good in. Though you can reach the saturation point with too much. Garrick Ohlsson worked for six months toward the 1970 Chopin competition in Warsaw. After he won, he said that he played nothing but Mozart for a month to launder his mind, and that it felt refreshing and great. I feel the same way after I've played the Rachmaninoff concertos a number of times—I have a need to play some early Beethoven. There are *so* many young musicians—the competition is so stiff—that perfectionism is the order of the day. You simply can't program something you play in a half-baked way. You're smart to stick to the things you do especially well. You have to capitalize on your strengths. I don't want to shove the rest away, though. There's still time for me to develop. I'll cautiously start programming other composers. I like Haydn very much. I relate more strongly to his sonatas than to some of the Mozarts—a choice that would shock a lot of musicians. I like the Haydns better as pieces, and they're not performed often. They're almost overlooked. I feel the attraction, and that perhaps helps me play them better. And the chamber-music experiences I've had have been invaluable. You learn to listen on a one-to-one basis—quite different from playing with an orchestra. It's a vital benefit to any young musician."

In some ways, Robin's New York début recital seemed too rich—for a non-pianist's blood, at any rate. Robin agreed that this was probably so, and said that if she had it to do over again she would not play all those great big pieces. She laughed. "It was my twenty-one-gun salute," she said. "At least I managed to omit the 'Appassionata.' I didn't want the critics to put me in the dust because I wasn't doing it the way they're used to hearing it. Actually, it's a good idea in a début to steer away from war-horses. I took a big risk playing the Chopin, because it's so overplayed. I was lucky with that piece, and, because of the good experience, I feel very secure with it now. If I'd gotten a bad review, I probably wouldn't have touched it again. Well, the New York début is the hardest thing for any musician to do. When you think of Alan and that bad review, and all the good things he's done since . . ."

Robin fell silent, but after a few moments she went on,
"The more I think about this business, the more important
personality seems to be. I don't mean charming an audience, though that counts. I mean getting along with people
and getting the most out of your relationships with them.
Especially the people you can learn from—the ability to be
with them and have them functioning at their best. When
I went to Mme. Kabos—the most tempestuous woman I
have ever met—I was new to New York and felt I was
treading water. I think if I'd had more ego strength I would
have learned more from her. In many ways, Mme. Dorfmann is an enigma to me—I suspect we get along because
my ego is stronger now. She tends to exaggerate when she
criticizes, and if you keep that in mind it's fine. She has
such an ear, and was a great performer. Now she's teaching
instead of playing, and I have a lot of empathy with her. Of
course, she can't help living vicariously through her pupils'
playing, and the result is that she's very demanding and
hard to please. But she has helped me a lot with sound. I
think about sound, and sound production, in a different
way because of her. She's such a tremendous person, and
when she is at her best there is no one equal to her. But you
have to catch her in the right mood."

Chapter 7

Robin came back to New York from her South American tour toward the end of June, and when I next saw her she told me that the trip had been quite an experience for her—high peaks while performing, a sense of estrangement when she woke mornings to hear an unfamiliar language outside her hotel window. "I played twelve concerts in twelve different cities and small towns," she said. "It was all very well organized. My plane was met at every city by an embassy or consulate man, and I was provided with a car and driver. There was always a small party after the concert. Still, it was lonely at times. The altitude affected me—the stewardess passed out coramine to everyone on the plane, but it wasn't very effective—and I didn't feel like sightseeing. Also, I was on my own a lot. One weekend, I was stuck in Piura, in northern Peru, for two days after the concert. I saw *El Gran Gatsby,* with subtitles, twice. But something nice happened there. The night of the concert, a young man came up to me backstage and presented me with an invitation, carefully typed in English: 'Very distinguished concert pianist: We would be very happy if you would come to give us an interpretation of your knowledgment at the piano. We are advancely thankful for your acceptation.' He was from a local music school. I went the next morning and played for them and talked, with the help of an interpreter."

Robin had some trouble in Arequipa—the second-largest city in Peru. According to her, the Arequipans have the reputation of being quite angry—even revolutionary—and during the intermission of her concert a young immigration man in chinos and dark glasses told her she would have to stop playing and come with him, because she had the wrong visa. "I needed a *visa artística,* because I was playing for money and, he said, taking soles away from Peruvians. I told him I was being paid in American dollars by my own country, but that didn't satisfy him. The American consul came backstage, but he was young and inexperienced and didn't know what to do. He went to make some phone calls, and the immigration fellow seemed ready to drag me off to jail. I figured he wouldn't arrest me onstage, so I dimmed the lights, went out, and finished the program. I certainly wasn't comfortable. He was waiting for me when I came offstage, but he'd softened somewhat. He said that I'd have to go down to immigration in the morning, and that I would be on 'personal parole' until I could get out of Arequipa. It was just a form of harassment. Ridiculous." She said that Arequipa had been bad news from the beginning. The hotel workers were on strike against government hotels the day she arrived. She took a nap before the concert, and when she woke the lights were off. There was no electricity. "I had trouble finding my contact lenses, and I was groping in the dark for the dress I'd planned to wear," she said. "Finally, I put all my clothes in a suitcase and took it to the concert hall and dressed there. What with the hassle just getting to the hall, and the arrogant kid from immigration, I was glad to get out of Arequipa."

I was curious to know what kind of audiences Robin had had, and she said, "Wonderful. The halls were always filled —anywhere from four hundred to twelve hundred people. The advertising was good—ads in papers and lots of posters. They were curious, of course, because I was not only American but a girl. They like to see women onstage; they have a high regard for them. The State Department did not specifically ask Juilliard to recommend a woman, though."

Remembering her bad experiences in New York, I asked what kind of pianos she had got, and she said, "I made out fairly well. I ran into a few P.S.O.s. When you get those, you just grit your teeth." I said I had read that Alicia de Larrocha had canceled a concert once because the piano was so bad, and Robin said, "At this point, I don't have that option, but an established artist like de Larrocha has every right to do so." In Trujillo, Robin thought she had struck gold. She went to the hall the afternoon of the concert to warm up. There was a nine-foot Bechstein—which many people feel is the Rolls-Royce of pianos—but when she opened the lid she found a mouse inside, eating the felt. She said she was glad that it happened before the concert. In Cuzco, she was invited to go from house to house to pick the best piano, and when she found one she liked, it was moved to the hall. The worst piano was in Ica. She had been promised a good one from the local university, but the students were on strike and wouldn't permit a piano to be moved out of the school—certainly not for an American pianist. "The man from the consulate met my plane, and the first thing he said was 'I hate to tell you this, but I don't think you're going to like the piano.' He took me straight to the hall, so I could have a look. There it was—the most ancient upright I'd ever seen. It looked like something my grandmother should have planted geraniums in. Unbelievable. I didn't even try it—I just said I'd be back at eight. Before the concert, I took the top off, so there would be a little more sound. I started the program with the Chopin Waltz in E Flat Major, the 'Grand Waltz.' There are quite a few low E-flats, naturally, and the first time I struck that key it stuck completely. I tried to raise it with my finger, but it was no go. So I stood up while I was playing, reached inside, and pulled the E-flat hammer up. The audience must have wondered what in the world I was doing. It kept happening, and when I stood the audience began applauding, and then cheering. It was a circus. Then I began rearranging—playing the E-flat an octave higher. I thought, Oh, God, if You just get me through this, I'll be *such* a nice person. All the bottom notes were bad. Some didn't sound at all. I cut a lot from that program. *No* repeats. I cut transition passages, entire sections. I'm glad it happened at the beginning of the tour. If it had been toward the end, I would have had to be carried off. Afterward, I had such a headache. That evening was really a horror—an absolute horror. I'm trying to put it out of my mind." But then the optimist in her surfaced, and she added, "It was probably one of the most won-over audiences I'll ever have."

Robin said she came to realize on the tour that one of the major challenges for a musician doing a number of concerts was trying to keep the playing fresh. "Toward the end, I began to think, Oh, my God, one more," she said. "I was so surprised at myself for feeling that way. But in retrospect I realize I shouldn't make a generalization based on that tour. There's a special loneliness—an anxiety—in a foreign country where you don't speak the language. I'll always remember my first night. The hotel room was cold, and I called the desk and tried to explain that I needed another blanket. I didn't think the desk man understood. Later, there was a knock on my door, and I was afraid to open it. I did, though, and it was a nice man with a blanket. But it was a major trauma for me."

That summer, after a vacation with her family, Robin returned to the Shawnigan Summer School of the Arts as a member of the faculty. This meant that she played a lot of chamber music, which included piano trios, quartets, quintets, and sonatas, many of them with the violinist Ruggiero Ricci, who has had an almost life-long successful career; many people consider him one of the all-time great violinists. He liked Robin's playing, and asked her to be his pianist. The distinction—"pianist" instead of "accompanist"—was hers, and one that she was entitled to make. The public's taste in music has broadened to such an extent that it is no longer interested only in a display of violin technique; there is a demand for meatier music—sonatas in which the pianist is an equal partner with the violinist. Robin, though she respects the difficulty and importance of accompanying, does not want to be anyone's accompanist.

Back in New York in the fall, in her small apartment in the West Seventies, Robin continued to work with Mme. Dorfmann. In October, she competed in the Naumburg Competition, as did Alan, who was still studying with Firkusny. Robin was one of ten semifinalists, in a strong field of eighty-five. Alan shared second prize with a pianist from Cuba. First place went to Dickran Atamian, from Texas. Competitions are proliferating, in almost direct ratio to the increasing number of musicians, and although the Naumburg is one of the most important, the *Times* did not announce the piano winner until after the vocal contest, more than a week later, and then it printed three paragraphs about the winning vocalists and, almost as an afterthought, named the pianist who had come in first. Several days after the Naumburg, I spoke with Robin, and it was one of the few times I found her depressed. "It's a bad business, no matter how you look at it," she said. "The healthy drives get obscured by realities. I'm getting to be almost an epicure of disillusion. I've had such tremendous hopes that I fear I'm beginning to wallow in the disappointments. I begin to feel that all unhappiness is mine alone." She stopped and thought, and then said, "There are *so* many young pianists coming up that sometimes I feel I'm in a great big stew, being stirred around. There's a rumor that Juilliard has already canceled its piano auditions for next March, because there are no places. Pianists seem to be coming out of the woodwork. I'm afraid to put a quarter in the Coke machine over there for fear a pianist will pop out playing the Chopin 'Double Thirds' Étude."

On November 16th, Robin and Alan and five other Concert Artists Guild contestants gave an all-Brahms chamber-music recital in St. Stephen's Church, on West Sixty-ninth Street. The C.A.G. had allowed Alan and Robin to pick a piano from the Steinway studio, on Fifty-seventh Street, and they were both thrilled. There were several rehearsals, and on Saturday morning, the day of the last, the seven young musicians arrived at the church to find the gate locked. They climbed over it, woke the rector, who let them in, and rehearsed in the cold building. The concert was well advertised and well attended. Between the trio Robin did, with violin and cello, and the quintet Alan played, with a string quartet, the two did ten Hungarian dances arranged for four-hand piano. Since Robin was warmed up and Alan was not, he cautioned her, in a whisper, to take it easy on the tempos until he was warmed up, too. The playing was joyous and affectionate.

At a post-concert party at Jane Harris's, Robin, Alan, and Richard Fields—who now had his own apartment, a new teacher, and the gleanings of serenity that went with a new sense of well-being—discussed a competition coming up in the spring. It was the big one—the Leventritt. Robin said that one really had to evaluate whether or not it was worth the effort. She was still irked at the Naumburg. Runners-up in that contest got no exposure—"not even a nursing-home concert," she said. Alan's prize was seven hundred and fifty dollars. "I don't want to sound ungrateful," he said, "but that's not much these days. I would have preferred a couple of concerts." The Leventritt, which is held at the whim of its director, Mrs. T. Roland Berner ("Talent is like shad—when it runs, it runs," she has said), with violinists and cellists one year, pianists another, was beginning to baffle everyone. Instead of competing with one another, the contestants were measured against certain standards, and in the past two competitions no first prize had been awarded. The concerts arranged for the finalists paid little, Robin said, and by the time a pianist had taken care of air fare and hotel room and bought something decent to wear, he would be lucky if he broke even. The Leventritt is closed to performers over twenty-eight, and since Robin had just turned twenty-six, and Alan would be twenty-six in two months, the upcoming Leventritt would be the last that either of them could enter. The congestion in the field was beginning to provoke acute anxiety in pianists in their mid-twenties; there were herds of younger pianists shoving their way to the fore—a little too old to be called prodigies but young enough to impress teachers and critics. In music, a performer gets more points for potential at twenty than at twenty-five, even though many very successful artists have not hit full stride until they were in their middle or late thirties, or sometimes older. And there is so much work involved in getting ready for a big competition—polishing special pieces to satisfy repertoire requirements, which have been getting stiffer and stiffer, while the rest of one's repertoire suffers. Still, after giving it a lot of thought, Robin sent an application to the Leventritt Foundation, and so did Alan.

Through the fall and winter, Robin continued to do solo concerts on the East Coast—in Connecticut, in North Carolina, in Washington, D.C.—and she was still playing any jazz dates that she could fit into her schedule. In January of 1976, she flew to Spokane to do the Tchaikovsky Concerto No. 1 with the Spokane Symphony, and the reviews were wonderful. The *Spokesman-Review* said, in part, "Magnificent . . . virtually awesome . . . first-rate concert pianist, and her stature will only increase with time. An electrifying performance . . . forceful and dramatic . . . playing with an intense passion . . . a master pianist both technically and emotionally." The *Chronicle* said, "A magnificent performance . . . brought the audience to life . . . music flowed from her piano, sweeping over the audience . . . always astute interpretation."

Robin played with Ricci in Carnegie Hall on March 14th. Their first appearance in New York together was, with the exception of a Busoni sonata, primarily a showcase for the violinist, and—though Ricci gallantly brought Robin out for repeated bows—the *Times* critic Donal Henahan treated it as such. He said Ricci was "capably assisted" by Robin, and she was disappointed at the review, and not reassured by Bloch, who said that her expectations of a more detailed mention in the review were unrealistic—that the emphasis of the recital was on Ricci and a display of his pyrotechnics, so of course the critic, no matter who it was, would concentrate on him.

In April, Robin went to Seattle to play the Rachmaninoff Second Concerto with the Seattle Symphony, and again got good reviews. The Seattle *Times* said, "Her control of the piano is exemplary, and her musicianship is consistently informed and tasteful. Moreover, she has that something—call it charisma—that is possessed by all topflight performers."

Late in April, Robin and Alan were both accepted as contestants in the Leventritt, scheduled for May, but meanwhile Robin had been invited to make another State Department tour in South America—an unusual circumstance, and proof that the first tour had been a success. She would have to concentrate on preparing for the tour, which would take her out of the country for the month of June. Her repertoire had grown to include fourteen concertos and four solo recitals, or about six hours of solo playing, but at the last minute, because of the Bicentennial, the State Department asked her to program two hours of American music. She played the Copland, which two years before she had felt was not a good piece for her, but it was a scramble to find more American pieces she liked.

One day early in May, Robin told me that she had written but hadn't mailed a letter to the Leventritt Foundation saying she would be unable to compete after all. Ricci had told her that his manager, Herbert Barrett, was looking for another pianist for his "stable," and that there was a chance Robin might be asked to audition for him. Barrett is considered one of the best in the business. He does not sign on more artists than his staff can adequately represent, and he would never represent anyone for a prepaid fee. His plan was that after he had found six pianists he would rent the Recital Hall and hear all six in one day. Getting ready for that audition, preparing all the American music, and working up the repertoire that would meet the Leventritt's requirements would be too much for Robin. "I've been carrying this letter around for a week," she said. "I hate to pass up the chance, but I can't do everything." In spite of the tour and the possibility of the Barrett audition, she seemed rather downcast. She said that at least she had found the right American music: in addition to the Copland sonata, she would play some Menotti, Barber, and Gershwin, a piece by Paul Tufts, a Seattle composer, and some Scott Joplin rags. She said, "I love the Copland—it's a beautiful piece. I learned it for the Naumburg, which is best forgotten." She would be playing a concerto with the National Orchestra of Peru, and she planned to do the Rachmaninoff Second. "The State Department also wanted the Gershwin *Rhapsody in Blue*, but I threw a fit," she told me. "I said, 'Please, *no*. I've been slugging out so many notes of American music I'm turning into a piece of apple pie.' Maybe I should drape myself in an American flag when I play." As she talked, she began to cheer up a bit, and the gloomy look changed to one of resolution. "Actually, I've been luckier in New York than I expected to be, though right now I want the Barrett management so much I can taste it. But I shouldn't be impatient. A boy at Juilliard won a very big new competition in Italy months ago, and he still doesn't have a manager." She said that a friend of hers was bitter about not having won the Naumburg, because he knew that he had played well. Robin told him that being bitter was not his prerogative. "That's what someone told me, and I thought it might help him to hear it," she said. "You have to become philosophical—there are too many intangibles at work. You have to try to take it just as philosophically when you win as when you lose." She paused, and then added, "Well, everyone's entitled to a little self-indulgence after one of these things. Twenty-four hours of self-pity, and that's it."

Robin said that that morning Dean Waldrop had told her there was an opening at the Diller-Quaile School of Music, in Manhattan, and he wanted to recommend her. "I was flattered, but I told him, 'I'm too young to die. I still want to practice and try a little longer. Then I'll be happy to do something like that.'" She said then that she was wasting valuable practice time, and, also, she wanted to mail the letter, put the Leventritt out of her mind. Before we parted, she said, "One thing I tell myself, one thing I've learned— everyone, even the greatest, has ups and downs, a streak of bad breaks, and it can be very hard on you emotionally. And if you don't get great gratification from music—love it in the right way—it can finish you."

Chapter 8

There are a lot of competitions in the spring—to the dismay of teachers and the deep distress of students. Many teachers abhor competitions in general. They limit repertoire growth, since students spend much too much time on certain pieces, and they are heartbreakers for the ninety-nine percent who will lose (in the case of the Leventritt, perhaps a hundred percent). Critics don't care for them, either. They feel that contests turn out contest players—note-perfect robots—rather than concert players. Still, both teachers and critics recognize that competitions do provide an opportunity for a student to gain recognition—managers send scouts to the big ones—and teachers do all they can to prepare their pupils for the ordeal. Probably only Horowitz could take a stand against them—as he did in July of 1976, when he said that he would accept two students to benefit the ailing Mannes College of Music, in Manhattan, on the condition that whomever he chose would promise not to enter any competitions. He said, in an interview in the *Times*, "I'm absolutely against competitions. In competitions, winners are chosen by elimination, not by excellence, and sometimes when the winner goes out on his own, there is not enough excellence. Also, sometimes it's political; it does not smell good."

Pianists who have come close but not won a contest might take cold comfort from the critic Andrew Porter's account of the 1969 Leeds International Piano Competition, in the London *Financial Times*. "This year the semifinals produced eight pianists all of remarkable equality," Porter wrote. "Which five were chosen to go on into the final round, and how those five were ordered, is not so important. Another round or a slightly different jury might have changed that order—and at one time, indeed, it was uncertain whether the eventual winner would even make the finals." For many young musicians, however, winning a big one seems the only door to a career, and they keep trying—hopping from one contest to another, New York to Leeds to Moscow to Fort Worth (where Cliburn now has his own competition), indefatigable and, most often, unrewarded. Thus, a pianist named Robert Benz appeared in Leeds in 1975, did not get past the semifinals of the 1976 Leventritt, and placed first in the Liszt-Bartók

International Piano Competition in Budapest four months later. The second-prize winner in that contest, Gary Steigerwalt, who also won an additional honor for his Bartók, had been one of the four Concert Artists Guild winners when Robin and Alan won, but he had been eliminated in the early stages of both the Naumburg and the Leventritt. (A rumor that neither of the winners at Budapest would be allowed to take his winnings out of Hungary proved, blessedly, to be false.)

For the 1976 Leventritt International Competition, Mrs. Berner, the daughter of Edgar Leventritt (in whose memory the competition was founded), announced that the first prize would be raised from a thousand dollars to ten thousand—matching the Cliburn Quadrennial first prize and evoking a momentary spasm of regret in Robin—and that all finalists would receive a thousand dollars; as usual, the winner would get a number of engagements with major orchestras. Mrs. Berner also hired the public-relations firm of Gurtman & Murtha to publicize the contest. (Sometimes it seems that competitions are competing with each other.) The Leventritt is considered so important because sixty percent of its winners have gone on to successful careers. (One of the exceptions was the 1954 winner, Van Cliburn, whose career was dormant until 1958, when he won the International Tchaikovsky Competition in Moscow and was honored with a ticker-tape parade up Broadway, briefly raising musicians to the popular level of presidents, aviators, and fired generals.) Everyone but the contestants said that the ten thousand dollars was insignificant—that the prestige and the orchestral appearances were what counted. Gurtman & Murtha was so successful in its assignment that it made the contest (if not actual front-page)

second-section front-page news in the *New York Times;*
probably even more important, as a result of the firm's
efforts, CBS-TV's "60 Minutes" decided to do a segment on
the Leventritt. No contest since the 1958 Tchaikovsky had
generated so much public enthusiasm.

The preliminaries were held in the WQXR auditorium,
on the ninth floor of the Times Building. Sixty-five pianists
(twenty had dropped out at the last minute) from eighteen
countries—a large number of them women—did the best
they could in approximately twenty minutes before a jury
of eight pianists that varied from day to day in name but
not in caliber. Throughout the competition, the contestants were allowed to warm up on a piece of their choice.
Then the judges requested works they would like to hear,
and in no case during the preliminaries and the semifinals
was the contestant allowed to finish a request. He might be
in the middle of a phrase, and be interrupted by a loud
hand-clap from the judge in charge of the jury—a different
one each day—with a request for the second movement of,
say, a Mozart sonata or the last movement of a Beethoven
concerto. Some felt the longer the judges let them play the
worse their playing got; it was so hard to put out of one's
mind the anticipation of that hand-clap.

Television lights had been set up in all corners of the
small auditorium, and there were lights on the stage as
well, trained on two Steinways, placed side by side. The
television crew men tried to be as unobtrusive as possible,
though throughout the preliminaries they signaled each
other when they wanted to stop the cameras and the sound
equipment positioned at the edge of the stage and blinking
red lights, like *Hal* in *2001*—with throat-slicing gestures:
chilling—under the circumstances.

The repertoire requirements included three concertos of different composers and periods plus ninety to a hundred and twenty minutes of solo works, again—representing different periods. The foundation provided an accompanist to play the piano reductions of the orchestral scores: Harriet Wingreen, a professional known for her exceptional musicianship, with Tom Muraco, another pianist, to spell her. They turned pages for each other. Miss Wingreen also worked with many of the contestants privately at night.

Peter Gelb, from Gurtman & Murtha, told me that a contestant from Uruguay was a strong contender because this was his third time around. Sixty-five pianists in seven days begin to numb anyone who isn't a pianist. I found myself reacting to their appearance rather than their playing: a big teddy-bear pianist who would have looked more believable on a football team playing with extraordinary sensitivity on an instrument whose size seemed diminished by the size of the performer; a thin pony-tailed blond in cork-soled platform shoes, the soles at least three inches high (How could she comfortably pedal? She left the auditorium after she played, clinging to the arm of a young man and so shaken that without his arm she might have collapsed); the Uruguay favorite, who came out with a confidence that suggested he already had the prize in his pocket; a French pianist who, with a show of nonchalance, stood and played a one-hand, two-octave scale, testing the piano, before he sat down to play.

When Alan came out, he seemed in remarkable control. He is an introspective pianist with a very personal style—very free with the instrument. He has a strong conception of what he's playing, and a good mind to back it up. He tends to orchestrate as he plays, bringing out the inner voices with subtle coloring. It's a compliment to say he's a musician first and a pianist second. His confidence and involvement in what he was doing were visible as he performed for the judges.

One of my favorites during the preliminaries was a lovely girl with shoulder-length brown hair, in a black and white polka-dot dress, who managed to simulate ease and grace and self-assurance while she played in the glare of the television lights for eight of the world's best musicians. We left the building together—she was the last of the day—and I congratulated her on her playing. She said, "Are you kidding? I *blew* it, I absolutely *blew* the concerto. Whew!" She stopped and took a deep breath. "I feel as if I've been through a car wash with no car." I asked if this was her first competition, and learned that she had gone at the contest game in a fairly helter-skelter way—the Tchaikovsky, the Concert Artists Guild, and now the Leventritt—and had never won anything. She was a graduate of the Eastman School of Music, in Rochester, New York, and did not currently have a teacher—she said she couldn't afford one and didn't want one. "They only make you play the way *they* play," she said. She lived with her family in New Jersey, and was on her way to the Port Authority Bus Terminal. I asked what her plans were—the next step—and she said firmly, "If I don't win this, I'm going to be a waitress."

The *Times* listed thirteen pianists who had made it to the semifinals, and Alan was included (the girl in the polka-dot dress was not). But Alan did not make it to the finals. (He later told me that he had psyched himself up for the preliminaries. When it came to the semifinals, he was emotionally drained, and hampered by the thought that he

must play even better than he had during the preliminaries
—a dangerous state of mind, he said, in which to try to
make an impact on the judges.) Of the five who made it,
three were women.

The finals were held on Wednesday, May 26th, at 11 A.M.,
in Carnegie Hall, and, as is customary with major competitions, they were open to the public and free. At ten that
morning, a large crowd of people had bunched under the
marquee of Carnegie Hall—as people attending an event
for which there are no reserved seats tend to do—waiting
for the doors to be opened, at ten-thirty. On the Seventh
Avenue side of the hall, a large, handsome poster—the
pride of Mrs. Berner—announced the day and time of the
finals, the information framed by a large L formed from
photographs of past Leventritt winners. The stage-door
entrance, on Fifty-sixth Street, was clogged with people:
members of the press, including representatives of A.P.,
U.P.I., the *Times, Newsweek, Time,* and several publications
devoted to music and musicians; TV cameramen and their as-
sistants; scouts from every major New York concert management; piano teachers from all over the Eastern seaboard;
Mr. Gelb and several others from Gurtman & Murtha;
Harriet and Tom, the former now transporting some forty-
odd concerto parts in a golfbag cart. An industrious, uniformed guard tried vainly to keep some kind of order.

Carnegie Hall inside looked especially grand that day. It
was the first time I had seen it in the morning, without
bright lights, bustling, chattering concertgoers, harassed
ushers. Instead, it was pleasantly serene. The front half of
the parquet was filled with early arrivals; the back half had
been roped off and reserved for the judges, the press, and
people well known in the music world. Uniformed ushers

stood behind the aisle ropes, guarding the reserved section. Television cameras had been set up in different sections of the dress circle, and lights were trained on the secluded central section where the judges sat and on the stage, which held two nine-foot Steinways, side by side, and two adjustable piano benches. Although the judges had spelled one another throughout the preliminaries and the semifinals, today they were all there, an unusually distinguished group to be assembled at the same time and in the same place: the pianists Rudolf Firkusny, Leon Fleisher, Sidney Foster, Claude Frank, Richard Goode, Gitta Gradova, Gary Graffman, Mieczyslaw Horszowski, William Masselos, Nadia Reisenberg, and Rudolf Serkin, and the conductors Max Rudolf and William Steinberg. Several of them were shielding their eyes against the glare of the lights. Rosalie Berner, clipboard in hand, was talking to her son Richard, who was sitting across the aisle from the judges; he had taken the day off from his law practice to lend a hand. Because of the distance between the judges and the stage, at the finals, instead of the judges calling to the contestants, Richard would relay the judges' requests to the contestants. The pianists agreed that it was a soothing arrangement—better than being shouted at.

The order in which the finalists would play had been determined by draw, and the first was twenty-seven-year-old Marian Hahn, from Greenwich, Connecticut. Her credentials included an M.A. from Juilliard; excellent reviews for two Carnegie Recital Hall appearances; first prize in a number of American competitions; and first in the Busoni in 1972. She had appeared with several orchestras, including the Cleveland.

Contestants were again allowed to begin with a piece of their choice, and since Miss Hahn had chosen the first movement of the Beethoven Concerto No. 5, she was followed onstage by Harriet and Tom. Miss Hahn was wearing a long-sleeved white turtleneck and a bright-orange floor-length skirt. Her walk was almost buoyant, and she seemed relaxed and at ease. This proved to be true of the four others as well. Perhaps since they had come this close and were already sure to receive a thousand dollars, the occasion was a joyous one instead of a tense, fear-inspiring test. After the Beethoven, the judges requested a Chopin Ballade and the second and third movements of the Schubert A-Major Sonata. Another nice thing about the finals: the contestants were allowed to finish each piece and hence did not have to worry about being interrupted. When she had finished, the audience applauded enthusiastically, calling her back for several bows.

Steven De Groote was next. Born in Johannesburg in 1953, De Groote had performed with orchestras in South Africa, Brussels, the Netherlands, and the United States. He now lives in Philadelphia, where he studied with Serkin and Horszowski at the Curtis Institute. Since both men were judges, in accordance with competition rules, they gave their votes to impartial colleagues and retreated to the back of the hall. De Groote, in a plaid jacket and tan slacks, appeared casual and relaxed—the clothes a contrast to the funereal dark suits that seemed to be the uniform for most of the preliminary players. He began with the Liszt Sonata, and then, at the judges' request, followed with the first and second movements of the Mozart Concerto in A Major. In the Mozart he demonstrated control and finesse, a subdued hall-hushing pianissimo, and a tenderness of touch, and I found myself thinking that he could win—if he was not too subdued. He concluded with the Chopin Scherzo No. 4 in E Major, Opus 54.

Late arrivals were allowed into the hall between numbers, and I noticed that the balconies were now filling up. Mr. Gelb managed unobtrusively to be everywhere at once. During De Groote's performance a man with a camera made it to the edge of the stage, on the far-right aisle, and was taking pictures. Mr. Gelb directed him up the aisle to the dress circle, where he knelt, taking pictures for the rest of the contest. Otherwise, the audience was one of the most quiet and attentive I'd seen in some time. A woman sitting next to me scrutinized the pianists through binoculars. Between numbers, she told me she was a piano teacher. "I came to the finals ten years ago, and it was nothing like this. They weren't as good then. The technique today is unbelievable."

It had been rumored throughout the competition that the next contestant, twenty-two-year-old Lydia Artymiw, of Philadelphia, had an excellent chance of placing first. Despite her youth, she had already performed with the Philadelphia Orchestra, the Buffalo and Baltimore Symphonies; had given solo recitals in Philadelphia, New York, Chicago, Washington, Rome, and Milan; was a participant in the Marlboro Music Festival in 1972 and 1974; and had toured nationally with Music from Marlboro groups. Furthermore, she already had a manager—Harry Beall Management. Her current teacher was Gary Graffman, and he relinquished his vote and went to the back of the hall. Miss Artymiw had chosen the first movement of the Rachmaninoff Concerto No. 1 as her first piece. She was wearing a blue short-sleeved, trim-waisted, knee-length dress, a style I'd seen so many times throughout the preliminaries that by now I felt I could spot a serious pianist in a crowded subway. Miss Artymiw played with some nondisturbing body English—head thrust forward at times, face lowered, as if attempting an intimate contact with the piano during softer passages.

The intent audience, the poise of the artists, the beauty of the music, the quality of the performances, the applause that prompted repeated curtain calls at times had lulled me into a feeling of being at a concert rather than a contest. Thus, as Miss Artymiw sat waiting for the judges' request, it was a shock when Harriet came onstage and brought her a glass of water. The judges were studying Miss Artymiw's contest repertoire, whispering to one another, finally nodding in agreement. Richard was told what they wanted to hear, and he dutifully trotted up the aisle to the stage and relayed the information. Harriet and Tom were beckoned onstage, so it was clearly to be a concerto. Tom took the accompanist's bench this time, and Miss Artymiw nodded at him. Both pianists raised their hands, and struck chords in unison. A shocking dissonance resulted. The audience laughed, pleased at the release in tension, at a dysfunction in this competition run with the precision of a Swiss watch. Tom had plunged into a Chopin concerto, whereas it was the third movement of the Beethoven Third that had been requested. Tom produced the correct music and the competition continued. During the Beethoven, Miss Artymiw had a memory lapse, but she made a quick recovery. Memory lapses have happened onstage to established musicians, and have not been considered all that crucial, but in a contest they can be fatal.

Santiago Rodriguez, born in Cárdenas, Cuba, in 1952, was the next to last contestant. His track record was impressive, too: honors in the Van Cliburn Quadrennial Competition in 1973 and the Tchaikovsky Competition in 1974; second prize in the 1975 Naumburg; soloist with orchestras throughout the United States and recitals in major cities, including Washington, Chicago, and New York. He had chosen the first movement of the Brahms First Concerto, and he was the only one who had brought his own accompanist. The audience was growing more and more enthusiastic, and Mr. Rodriguez' Brahms drew an exceptionally intense reaction. Shouts of bravo were mixed with the applause. Mr. Rodriguez finished with the Mozart C Minor Sonata and the last movement of the Beethoven Third Concerto.

The final contestant was twenty-eight-year-old Mitsuko Uchida, born in Tokyo and currently living in London. She had won first prize in a number of competitions, and placed second in the prestigious Leeds; had made orchestral appearances all over Europe; had a number of Toshiba-EMI recordings to her credit; and in 1972 had won the Fukuyama Award as the best Japanese pianist of the year —no small achievement. She was by far the most experienced of all the contestants, and the oldest the competition would admit. Miss Uchida had chosen the first movement of the Chopin Sonata in B Minor as her first piece, and she walked out alone. She is a stunning, porcelain-skinned woman, and she came out with poise and confidence and a bright smile, wearing a long, full, elegant dress of black silk, scattered with huge orange poppies, with thin shoulder straps that revealed graceful shoulders and slim arms. Her hair was straight, long, fine, and as black and silken as her dress. The TV cameras angled in closer. There was something about the fluidity of her movement, her grace, the yielding dress that contributed to an illusion that the piano had ceased to be a percussion instrument. Her playing had lyricism, warmth, dramatic contrasts, and none of the proverbial Oriental cool. Since she clearly understood the limitations of the instrument, there was an absence in bravura passages of murky reverberations—present, at times, in Mr. Rodriguez' Brahms. While she waited for the judges' request, she turned the knobs of the piano bench to raise it an inch or so. "Mind Your Musical Manners," an Emily Post-type book on competition behavior, sternly tells contestants to do such adjustments before beginning to play, but some do not, fearing they might appear nervous or waste valuable time. The judges asked for the second movement of the Chopin and she concluded, at their request, her part of the competition with the Beethoven Concerto No. 3, with Tom as her accompanist. They did it with great style and high spirits. Miss Uchida acknowledged the applause, and the contest was over.

The judges made their way up to the Green Room, trailed by several cameramen. The audience crowded along the footlights and up the aisles, as if they'd get the results faster from a closer position. The corridor leading to the backstage area was jammed. The uniformed guard was at last having some success; he was keeping people from coming through the glass doors that led to the backstage area. Raymond Ericson, from the *Times,* was there, and I asked him if he had a favorite. He was noncommittal, but said, "I never heard the Liszt Sonata played more beautifully than

Mr. De Groote did it today." He paused a second, and then added, "Though I don't know why any pianist would want to play it. It's so boring." A jaunty-looking man in a sporty tan suit asked me if I was rooting for someone, as though we were at Aqueduct or Madison Square Garden. I asked if he was a musician, and he said, "No. I just read about it in the paper, and the wife and I drove over from Jersey. It was a lot of fun, and besides, it was free." Harriet was at the water cooler outside the glass doors, and I asked her who she thought the winner would be. She said, "The Japanese girl, hands down." I started to ask if she had any idea how long it would take for the judges to arrive at a decision—this was not her first Leventritt—when the ever-present Mr. Gelb opened the doors to the auditorium, stuck his head out, and said the judges had reached a decision.

I said goodbye to Harriet and went back into the hall. TV cameras were being carted onstage by crews that seemed to be multiplying. A floor microphone was brought onstage and tested by Mr. Gelb. The judges came on, single file, followed by the five contestants, Mrs. Berner, and a man in a conservative suit and a flamboyant tie. He stepped up to the mike, introduced himself as the city's Deputy Commissioner of Culture. He was there, as Mayor Beame's representative, to present Mrs. Berner with a plaque in honor of her hard work and the Leventritt Competition's great contribution to cultural life in the city. Mrs. Berner accepted the plaque, thanked the Deputy Commissioner and Mayor Beame, thanked the judges and introduced them individually to the audience, and then she said, "As you know, each finalist in the Leventritt receives a prize of one thousand dollars, plus a three-year management contract and appearances both in recital and with orchestras. The judges have decided that this year there will be no first prize." The audience responded with boos and hisses and no applause, and during a momentary stunned silence a man was heard to say, "That's one way to save ten thousand dollars." But onstage, grace, courtesy, and courage prevailed. Mrs. Berner, tears in her eyes, embraced each contestant; judges shook hands with one another, an occasional laugh indicating an exchange of anecdotes; the TV crew packed up their equipment, and the audience, audibly disgruntled, left.

I went out the Fifty-seventh Street exit and around the corner to Seventh Avenue to have a final look at the Leventritt poster Mrs. Berner was so proud of. The poster was no longer there. It had been replaced by one announcing a coming attraction.

Rumors in the music world were that although the pianists had been good, ten thousand dollars was a lot of money (one week earlier, the twenty-six-year-old Mark Hayes had won, by two strokes, forty thousand dollars in the Byron Nelson Golf Classic), and none of them had been that good; that because of all the publicity the judges didn't want to commit themselves, to risk picking someone who would prove to be an embarrassment (some Leventritt winners have not gone on to major careers, and have dropped from sight); that no one of the contestants was truly good enough to sustain an instant career.

Several days later, I called Mrs. Berner. She was still upset. I asked if she had favored any of the contestants, and she said, "They are always all my favorites. Maybe now you'll understand why I can't have the contest every year. I might never do it again." Next, I called Mr. Murtha to congratulate him for the way the competition was run, which was largely a result of his and Mr. Gelb's industry and respect for the musicians. He admitted that he was disappointed in the results. I said I'd had high hopes for Mitsuko Uchida, who was now too old for another Leventritt. Murtha said, "It should please you to know, then, that she just this minute signed a contract in my office with the Harold Shaw Management." He paused and added, "As for the others, there's always another year, another competition, another chance." His words were prophetic. The following year, Steven De Groote won first prize at the Van Cliburn Quadrennial—with, for the first time in the competition's history, a judges' decision that, while controversial, was virtually unanimous.

Time and *Newsweek* printed nothing about the competition, but "60 Minutes" went ahead with its program, which was shown at the beginning of September. The only snag the TV crew encountered was getting some of the contestants to agree to be filmed while calling the foundation to find out whether they had made the semifinals. A number flatly refused, but three finally agreed. Although she wasn't named on the program, there was a lot of footage of the girl in the polka-dot dress just before she went out to play. She was wearing black gloves, to keep her hands warm, and she was shrugging and laughing helplessly. She said, "I wish I could vanish—evaporate."

During the Leventritt finals, Robin was next door, in Carnegie Recital Hall, auditioning for Herbert Barrett and his five salespeople. Although the audition was closed to outsiders, several scouts from the Leventritt slipped in to listen, and one of them whispered to Barrett, "I didn't hear anything this good next door." After the audition was over, Barrett told Robin he would let her know his decision in a few days. The following Wednesday night, Robin and Richard Fields stopped by to see me. They had been celebrating with champagne. That afternoon, Barrett had called Robin down to his office to sign a contract. Her cheeks were pink and there was a sparkle in her eyes, and she told me that she had played very, very well at the audition. Robin had always been her own severest critic, and it was the first time since I had met her that she had ever said any such thing.

Robin and Richard talked about the Leventritt. They seemed to know quite a few of the contestants, and Robin said of a French pianist, "He already has a good career in Europe. Losing this can only hurt him." He was rumored to be a favorite of the judges in the preliminaries, but in the semifinals he seemed very tired, his playing did not hold up, and he was eliminated. (Everyone at Juilliard was only too aware of the case of a young pianist who had signed with a major manager who urged him to enter a Leventritt; when he entered and didn't win, the manager dropped him.)

Richard said that he was now busy accompanying some of Juilliard's best violinists in master classes and recitals. He was finally getting some recognition and acclaim, and his air of self-defeat had virtually vanished. Robin was urging him to enter next year's Concert Artists Guild competition.

They said they had to leave, and while they were putting their coats on, Robin told me, "Firkusny was complaining to me today about all the Mostly Mozart concerts he's scheduled to do in August. He said he would be practically living in Tully Hall." She laughed and added, "I told him he could at least count on a good stove. Many a goose has been cooked on that stage."

Chapter 9

Reputable managers open doors. Conductors deal with them, and not with the individual musician—contrary to the thirties Hollywood image of a young Deanna Durbin bursting into an orchestra rehearsal and screaming, "Mr. Stokowski! Mr. Stokowski! You must listen!" Movies of the thirties and forties outdid even themselves when it came to the subject of musicians. Several come to mind: Robert Taylor, conducting an orchestra in Moscow in a Tchaikovsky symphony, brings his wife, Susan Peters, onstage and onto the podium for the last movement, conducting with one arm and embracing her with the other. And John Garfield as a poor, struggling violinist who happens to be at an elegant cocktail party and also happens to have his violin with him, plus an invisible hundred-and-ten-man orchestra to accompany him, when Joan Crawford taunts him into playing. It is hard to imagine any pianist surviving—or for a moment submitting to—the whacks across the knuckles with a cane that Ann Todd accepts from James Mason; his hitting her there, of all places, makes no sense at all. Then there is the more recent, hilarious *The World of Henry Orient*, in which two adolescents have an implausible crush on a concert pianist—a pianist so inept that in real life he would not be permitted to play with a bad amateur orchestra. And there are current examples as well: in the 1978 movie *Fingers* Harvey Keitel plays a role described by a Hollywood columnist as a "neurotic concert pianist," who practices frantically for the concert stage, taking time off occasionally to be the hit man for his father, a Mafia loan shark.

Impresarios, who are, after all, managers, don't wear black cloaks and opera hats and look like George Sanders, if Herbert Barrett is typical. They are indistinguishable from lawyers or accountants or bank vice-presidents. They are businessmen, and music is a business—and, given its emotional components, a well-run one. There are, of course, some managers whose tactics are highly suspect, but the same can be said of literary agents, doctors—people in almost any profession.

Barrett is a middle-aged man with gray-brown hair, dark-rimmed glasses, and a direct manner. He is not unfriendly, is even congenial, but in talking to him one is struck by his choice of words, his ability to come to the point. A week or so after Robin signed her contract, I called on him in his office, on the seventeenth floor of a building at Broadway and Sixty-first Street. It is a vast, cheerful place, with yellow walls, a tweed rug, several abstract prints, and, just inside the door, an enormous floor-to-ceiling evergreen tree. Behind his large oak desk, on top of the air conditioner, are five small ivy plants, visibly struggling for life. I was reminded of the wide range of musicians Barrett represents. After pulling up a chair for me, Barrett said, "To begin with, I'm pleased that we're representing Robin McCabe. I had a very good feeling, as we all did in the office, when I heard her play."

Robin had referred to the five people who had been present at her audition with Barrett as "salespeople," and I asked Barrett if that was indeed what they were called. "Without making it sound too flossy, basically we are all impresarios," he said. "Everyone here is a manager, who is interested in developing careers. However, we do call them salesmen, or salespeople, or sometimes scouts." He said that everyone had reacted to Robin with enthusiasm. "We had been primed beforehand, of course. We have represented Mr. Ricci for many years, and we respect his opinion very much. He told us that he had been playing with Robin in Canada, and that he thought she was a winner. We heard her play with him in Carnegie Hall and were impressed. And then we had her play for us in the small hall. Before that, we'd had very enthusiastic endorsements from Rudolf Firkusny, whom we do not manage but whom we respect very much, and letters from the higher echelon at Juilliard, including Dean Waldrop, who also called me. In other words, I rely on people whose judgment I respect, who know more about technique and musicianship than I do. When Robin was about to become part of our family, we had been indoctrinated. And that, essentially, is how we choose. First, by the time they come to us—those who want major management—they are ready for careers. They have years of work and many performances under their belt. Their teachers are always enthusiastic—if they weren't, they wouldn't have been working with those particular pianists. Their techniques are formidable, and they have all that experience behind them. Then the question is—a very subjective question—whether the charisma is there. I think it is essential, and you can tell if a performer has it, no matter whether the audience is very knowledgeable or has come simply to hear a performance, as it would come to a film or the theatre, and you know pretty quickly whether the audience is reacting to the person onstage. It's not just talk. There is something very specific about that cosmo-magnetic fluid that flows between the performer and you and has you sitting on the edge of your seat. Charisma takes different forms. Some major artists come onstage looking like Uriah Heep, and others come out with this enormous élan, like Rubinstein. When he hits a wrong note, he looks around almost proudly, as if he were saying, 'Look what *I* did.' Maybe it boils down to having a powerful personality. Whatever it is, we all feel quite strongly that Robin has it."

I had shown a Barrett brochure, containing pictures of his artists, to a pianist friend, who looked at the lineup and said, "They'll eat Robin alive." (Some are unknown to the general public but are considered giants-to-be in the music world.) When I told Barrett about this reaction, he said, "The curious thing about this business is that, if we have a very successful instrumentalist, instead of hurting the others it helps them. People who book artists come to us for more of the same. We managed Wilhelm Backhaus—one of the giant ones—and it helped all the other pianists on our list, because it made everyone conscious that Barrett management signified quality. So I think basically—especially with pianists, who are far and away the most popular instrumentalists for selling—the bigger stars help the smaller ones." He said that in terms of demand, violinists ran a relatively poor second to pianists, and cellists a poor third, and that this was probably as it should be, since pianists outnumbered the others.

It had become clear that orchestral appearances were extremely valuable for performers, and I asked Barrett if his firm was able to arrange them for his artists. He said, "Well, we know all the conductors, and we arrange auditions for the artists, and the rest is up to the artist. Conductors aren't apt to audition someone who does not come recommended by management or by a *very* successful musician or fellow-conductor. As for solo recitals, our salespeople spend a certain number of weeks on the road promoting them. What has happened in the business, if you want a little bit of the background, is that twenty or twenty-five years ago there were a number of local managers in cities throughout the country who risked their own capital, or that of clubs or associations that they guided, to put on concerts by solo artists. Then, as each manager either retired or died, instead of being replaced by another local manager, he was replaced by a university. Each university has its own concert series, providing concerts for its students and also for the surrounding communities. For instance, in 1954 Boston University became the sponsor of

Aaron Richmond's Celebrity Series. A university today has a person who is the equivalent of a professor, or a football coach, except that he's the director of cultural activities. Twenty or twenty-five years ago, music departments were often relegated to some side street off campus, somewhere near the pharmacy school. Now universities are building arts centers—each more opulent than the next. And it is to the directors of cultural activities that our salesmen address themselves, trying to convince them that the Robin McCabes are the Horowitzes of the future."

I asked Barrett if managements such as his provided publicity for their artists, and he said that those expenses were paid for by the artists. He said, "There's no denying the value of publicity, but you have to have something to publicize, and at this point Robin doesn't. A South American tour isn't enough. But if a winner of a major competition doesn't have an expert p.r. man poised for action, all his success can too soon be forgotten. Soon everyone will be talking about next year's winner, and there are so many new, important competitions. Not too many years ago, a big-competition winner would have a choice of managers. Now, unless he has a good press, which he most often pays for himself, he might not get a nibble." Robin thinks an artist is lucky to have his name become a household word, and many printed stories about performers have been planted by a p.r. firm. Donal Henahan says such stories as "At Home with the Misha Dichters" might prompt someone to try the Dichter recipe for lasagna, but not necessarily go to a concert to hear him play.

I had heard that many musicians, no matter how experienced, were tortured by stagefright, and I asked Barrett if any of his artists were afflicted with it to such an extent that they didn't enjoy playing. "They *all* suffer, but they all enjoy playing," he said emphatically. "I've been in the business many years, and I don't know any artist who isn't scared before going onstage. Backhaus certainly was. He was one of the most organized people I ever met. For his hobby, he liked to study railroad timetables—he was that precise. But when he gave a concert here, after a number of years' absence, he was terrified. Rubinstein was backstage with him, saying, 'Go *on!*' and trying to push him onstage."

Reluctantly, I brought up the subject of money, but Barrett said, "You can talk about money—I live by it. An established artist can command as much as ten thousand dollars a performance. A newcomer, like Robin, would get a thousand. We don't bother with smaller fees. A thousand dollars is rather good for a pianist, but for a violinist, who has an accompanist to pay, double air fares, and hotel bills, a thousand dollars is no longer a thousand dollars."

In recent years, more and more women have become prominent on the music scene. They suffer no physical inferiority to men—as in sports—and, as the four-foot-nine-inch Alicia de Larrocha proves almost every time she performs, they can often outplay them. Even before women's lib, critics stopped saying of a woman performer, "She plays like a man"—which at one time was the highest accolade they could come up with. I had discussed the gradual increase in the number of women performers with various people. One critic suggested that women used to become discouraged early and quit to marry and have families. A psychiatrist felt that until recently women were not encouraged to flaunt the kind of ego essential to a performer. A public-relations woman mentioned "the ladies"

—women went to matinées and took their husbands to evening concerts, and they would rather watch a man perform than a woman.

Five of the nine pianists Barrett has under contract are women, and before I left I asked him to explain the phenomenon. "I took them on because they were the best I'd heard at the time," Barrett said. "I surprised myself. I counted them up and said, 'Well, I really *am* liberated.'"

Robin signed a three-year contract, and was told that if she proved to be a "repeater"—was asked back again and again—there was every reason to expect a fairly successful career. Barrett told me it was not possible to predict who would be a repeater. "It's a funny thing," he said. "It's almost traditional that when an artist plays a concert somewhere they say very nice things about him, and he comes back to us and, very sincerely, tells us he was loved in that particular town, and I'm sure he was. It's part of the affable, convivial, enthusiastic reaction that follows a concert. But sometimes he will be almost immediately forgotten. At least, he isn't asked back. The test is in the actual repeating of performances. And that involves more than talent and charisma. It has to do with the feeling of the audience that the artist *cares*—that he is enjoying being there. It may seem petty, but it's important that he remember the birthday of someone there, or that he go to the post-concert party, which looms very large in some communities, or that he take the time to hear some of the young hopefuls. All kinds of things. But most of all it's the excitement that he generates and whether it will last long enough for them to remember him and ask him back."

When Robin returned to New York in the fall of 1976, she found an apartment in a building filled with musicians, and Juilliard provided her with a Steinway grand; no more Sunday scrambles looking for a piano to practice on. She was slimmer and more chic than when I had first met her. The demure dresses had been replaced by trim slacks and sleek black turtlenecks, and she was wearing a handsome suede coat. Robin had completed all the work toward her doctor's degree except the dissertation, and she was still teaching at Juilliard and working on her own repertoire, which included more and more chamber music for concerts with Ricci. The two made frequent trips out of town to give recitals—sometimes joined by a cellist for a program of trios. Barrett had begun arranging auditions for Robin with different conductors, but, because music seasons are planned one or two years in advance, she couldn't expect many concerts through Barrett until the fall of 1977. She could expect to be asked occasionally to fill in for another pianist, and on Wednesday, December 1st, she got a call from Tittica Roberts, a vice-president of the Barrett firm. William Masselos was scheduled to play the Mozart K. 482 with the St. Paul Chamber Orchestra, in Minnesota, the following Saturday night, but he was sick. Was the concerto in Robin's repertoire and was she free that night? There are around twenty Mozart piano concertos, and K. 482 was one of those that Robin plays. She was going to give a concert with Ricci in Dallas on Monday, but she could change her plane ticket and go to St. Paul first. Miss Roberts said that the arrangement wasn't definite, and she would call back. Robin would have liked her first Barrett date to be less haphazard, but who knew when the next chance would come? She got out the music for K. 482 and began going over it. Late in the afternoon, Miss Roberts called back and said that the St. Paul Chamber Orchestra had gone to a different manager and picked a pianist who was considered a consummate Mozart interpreter—Rudolf Firkusny.

Robin told me about this on a Saturday in January. She was going to Baltimore the following Monday to audition for the conductor of the Baltimore Symphony, and she had spent the day at Juilliard practicing on a piano with a very stiff action. She wasn't knocking the piano on loan from the school, she said—she was delighted to have it—but the action was very loose. "If I blow on it, the keys go down."

I asked about Richard Fields and Roman and Alan. Richard had, on the spur of the moment, gone to Vienna to study. He felt he needed some time for reflection, a chance to strengthen himself, become more independent. He told Robin that Juilliard's neon-lit halls were no place for a young man to spend his youth. Roman, who had got his degree, was working at Juilliard as an accompanist. Alan was completing work for his doctorate and practicing harder than ever. He was gradually beginning to get more concerts.

In March, Juilliard held piano auditions after all, and Robin's sister Rachelle flew to New York to audition. Bloch had met her in Puyallup two years earlier when he went to Seattle to hear a production of the *Ring* cycle in English and reported that she was bright and personable— lovely, too. On the basis of their experience with Robin, both Firkusny and Mme. Dorfmann were interested in her, so it was no surprise to anyone that she was accepted.

In early May, the girl in the polka-dot dress whom I had met at the Leventritt called and told me what she'd been up to. She had, as she had said she would, become a waitress. But she continued to practice and she saved her money, and she rented Carnegie Recital Hall for May 14th, at 5:45 P.M., and paid Norman J. Seaman a modest sum to publicize her début recital. Hedging her bets and bucking the system, she used the name Lily von Ballmoos and revealed nothing about her background in the flyers or the recital program. The *Times*, proving that it does indeed cover all events, sent John Rockwell. He seemed bemused at the mystery surrounding the performer, and the unusual name, but he gave her a great review. She said she had received no offers from any managers, and now she was looking forward to a summer at Tanglewood, playing nothing but chamber music.

Late in May, Robin dropped in to say goodbye. She was leaving in a few days to give a concert in California, and then she would go to Washington for a week at home and on to Idaho for a vacation at her family's cottage, before going back to Canada for another season as a faculty member at Shawnigan.

I asked how the audition for the conductor in Baltimore had gone, and she laughed and said, "It was a fiasco. I was on a treadmill of talent being whisked past the conductor. He was obviously trying to fulfill all his commitments in one day. We were each allowed approximately twelve minutes in which to make an indelible impression. If he liked my playing, he'd get in touch with Mr. Barrett. I must admit, I felt for a while as if I were in a nightmare version of a competition." If she had once been "highly demolishable," clearly she no longer was. The Barrett contract seemed to have given her a sense of security, a knowledge that no single experience would be the end of her, a feeling that there was a lot to look forward to.

I asked Robin if, now that she had a manager, she would settle permanently in New York. She thought for a minute and said, "I think I could live in the Northwest and still have a career. There's no reason Mr. Barrett couldn't book concerts for me anyway; I wouldn't have to live in New York for that. And I could teach there, too. I love it there so much I can't imagine living any place else."

Chapter
10

When Robin returned to New York in the fall of 1977, she seemed almost transformed. She looked radiant, not at all girlish, and there was a new poise, a sense of confidence about her. She'd had an exciting and enriching summer at Shawnigan. She had a manager now, and was most definitely a professional. Although she had taught at Shawnigan other summers, possibly she felt that this time no one would confuse her with a student. She likes teaching, and is clearly good at it. (During the coming year, two students she had taught at Shawnigan would come to New York from Indiana and Toronto for lessons with her.) She said, "Shawnigan was wonderful this summer. Most of my pupils were really good. I had the chance to play lots of chamber music, and the faculty was unusually lively. Abbey Simon was there, and we became good friends. We played tennis as often as we could fit it in." She had a mischievous look on her face. "The games were vicious. He's a good player, but I sometimes beat him. Often we played doubles with people who were better than we were." She laughed. "By the end of the match, we usually brought them down to our level."

She said life would be as hectic as ever, but more varied than in the past. She had a number of concerts to play with Ricci all over the country, and she was determined to finish her dissertation, on "The Maturation of Liszt as a Composer as Shown Through His Revisions."

Throughout the fall and into the following spring she had sporadic meetings with her thesis adviser "whenever we both could get together." She had a gaggle of pupils at Juilliard, teaching in the Secondary Division, and quite a few private students. And she hoped to find time to work toward increasing her repertoire. She had also applied to the Martha Baird Rockefeller Fund for a grant to help pay for an Alice Tully Hall recital. Barrett felt the sooner she played in New York the better.

Early in November she was introduced to Seymour Solomon, president of Vanguard Records, at a cocktail party at Abbey Simon's. Simon, a lively, handsome, humorous man, is one of the greats in the piano world. (One fan trudged through sleet and snow to hear Simon play Schumann's *Carnaval* and reported to a friend that it was an experience he would probably tell his grandchildren about.) Simon told Solomon that if Vanguard needed another pianist in its stable, they couldn't find anyone better than Robin— that she was a brilliant pianist.

In the middle of December, Solomon called Robin and asked her to come to the Vanguard studios to do a demo tape for him and his brother, Maynard. (Robin had said to Simon, "I hope you didn't have to sell your soul to get me this," and he had replied, "I would never risk my own skin for *any*one. I recommended you because I believed what I told Seymour to be true. All I did was grease the wheels for you. You *are* a brilliant pianist. Now you'll have a chance to prove it at Vanguard.") In the interim, she'd had her first Barrett dates: on December 3rd an all-Chopin concert in Milwaukee with two other Barrett artists. Robin played a solo sonata, did a cello and piano sonata with Robert Sylvester, and accompanied Marianna Paunova in a group of songs. On December 7th and 8th she did the Liszt Concerto No. 1 with the Fort Lauderdale Symphony, and got a standing ovation both nights. And on December 12th she went to the Vanguard studios.

"Seymour and his brother and several other people were in the control room that overlooks the studio. I must say, I felt quite nervous. They really put me through my paces. For almost four hours I played every composer known to man. I started with pieces of my own choice, and then began playing ones they wanted to hear. I hadn't known what to expect, and was surprised at the variety of their requests—all the different composers. And then they began ticking off the big Beethovens, one by one. They asked for parts of the 'Waldstein,' the 'Pathetique,' the 'Moonlight.' I was baffled, and said to myself, 'What's going on here?

What do they want? How much do they want to hear anyway?' During the 'Moonlight,' I suddenly segued into an arrangement of 'Night and Day,' which fits into the harmony and triplet figures of the sonata—no deviation from the sonata's harmony—and Seymour flicked the switch that enabled him to talk to me in the studio. He was laughing, and he said, 'O.K., we'd heard you play jazz. Let's hear some now.' I played jazz for half an hour—it's all on tape!"

Wheels—even greased wheels—turn slowly in the record world, and it was not until February 24th that Seymour Solomon called Barrett and said Vanguard wanted to sign Robin—a five-year contract, with the number of recordings to be decided later.

The Martha Baird Rockefeller Fund for Music aids symphonies, opera companies, chamber groups, other ensembles, including an outfit called Bring Your Own Pillow, Inc., which in 1977 received $3,250 for electronic equipment to be used by the San Francisco Contemporary Players. It also aids individuals, young artists in their twenties and early thirties who, according to the application form,

> are in genuine need of assistance toward advancing their professional careers. Grants are approved on the basis of the applicant's professional training and experience, and the judgment of the Fund's Advisory Panel, following an audition in person, as to the candidate's artistic qualifications and the probable value of the plan for which he requests assistance. Auditions are intended as individual evaluations, not as competitions. The amount of a grant (from $1,000 to $3,500) will vary according to individual needs, based on the estimated cost of the plan proposed, and the personal resources of the applicant. Applications favorably recommended by the

Advisory Panel will be reviewed by the Trustees of the Fund.

The Fund is flooded with applications from aspiring performers, and the majority are not even considered. Those accepted are expected to be already into a career to a certain extent, to have a performance record that would indicate that, with some help—one more push—they could go far in their field. Robin was one of nine pianists chosen in 1977 to audition, and on December 14th, a windy, freezing day, she went down to Tully Hall to play for a panel of six judges. She offered them six big works, and the judges, as in a competition, chose bits and pieces from each. Robin couldn't see who the judges were because of the footlights, but she naturally hoped at least one of them was someone she knew. She later heard that the Fund wisely chose as judges not just pianists but singers and string players as well, feeling that a pianist, in spite of himself, will listen with a prejudiced ear. This way, the Fund would get a cross section of reactions.

Robin spent the holidays with her family, and when she returned to New York there was a letter waiting from the Martha Baird Rockefeller Fund asking her to come down to their offices, at Rockefeller Center, on January 9th, for an interview with Maude Brogan, the director of the Fund.

Miss Brogan, whom Robin described as being in her mid-forties, slim and attractive, with brown hair, showed Robin a typed summary of the judges' comments about her playing: "Beethoven—Liked first movement, though questioned the tempo. Beautiful sound." "Chopin—Very good, very strong." "This pianist obviously has a big technique. Is not afraid to take risks. Would recommend her for MBR help." "Tends to get percussive in the base when excited." "Not enough contrast in texture in the Haydn."

Robin said, "I immediately reacted inwardly to the comments, but I tried not to show panic. Miss Brogan sensed it, though, and she said, 'Remember, when a jury is compelled to write down reactions, they are going to want to write negative things.' Actually, the good far outweighed the bad. I realized later that during the interview, she played devil's advocate with me. The questions she asked were not antagonistic but the kind that arouse a big response in you: 'What are your mother and father like?' 'Whom do you relate more strongly to?' Unexpected in this type of interview. I think she was baiting me, trying to find out my true feelings in a short period of time. She asked me why I played transcriptions—of Schubert songs, for instance. In defense of transcriptions, in general, I said, 'Liszt was a wonderful transcriber, and if he hadn't transcribed the Beethoven symphonies for piano, there were many small towns where the symphonies would never have been heard at all.' She rightly said, 'Well, of course that's no longer true.'" Robin laughed and said, "I told her, 'Let me put it another way. I'm a pianist. I love the piano. I revel in what the piano can do. Transcriptions are piano music for the sake of the piano, and that's it. A glorification of the instrument. Not as serious as works written for the piano, that's true. But they're a tremendous novelty—done in proportion.' Then she asked me why I felt I deserved a recital. I told her, 'I'm at a point in my career where it would be of great importance to me. I think during the past couple of years I've demonstrated steady progress as far as my musicianship goes. I have an overall positive feeling about my growth as an artist.' Miss Brogan took notes, and was friendly in manner. I left the interview with no feeling one way or another about whether or not I would get a grant."

Throughout the year, when Simon, Robin, or Bloch was working on a concerto and wanted to rehearse it with another pianist playing the piano reduction of the orchestral score, the three helped one another out. Robin did the seldom-played Delius with Bloch—who was scheduled to play it with the Louisville Symphony at a Romantic Music Festival in Indianapolis in April—and the Rachmaninoff First with Simon, who would play it with the New York Philharmonic in the near future. She was building her own repertoire, practicing whenever she had some free time, and when she had worked up the Gershwin Concerto in F Major (written after the *Rhapsody in Blue* and the composer's only attempt at writing in a formal musical structure), she asked Simon to read through it with her. He'd played the solo part countless times, and might even give her a few pointers. I went along to listen.

They met in Simon's studio one morning—he had a free hour before his first student would arrive—and got to work almost immediately. Chelle, a lovely blue-eyed blond, was there, to turn pages for Simon. He had left his glasses at home, and before beginning he squinted at the score and said, "This might not sound like what Gershwin had in mind, but I'll do my best."

The first movement, an allegro, has jazz and cakewalk rhythms throughout, with contrasts between grandiose, full-orchestra passages, solo-piano statements, and slow, rhapsodic sections where the piano is in dialogue with the orchestra. The work begins with the orchestra in full force, with a crashing chord that makes way for the entrance of the solo piano—a two-octave glissando beginning on a low C that almost sidles into a D-flat, a poignant resolution that Simon said should "send a shiver up the spine." Throughout the session, they continued to play as they talked, stopping only occasionally to discuss a point.

Simon said of her opening glissando, "Don't push. Just wallow in it. And I would play the second phrase straighter than you do."

Robin said, "You have to feel svelte and sexy for Gershwin," and Simon said, "That lets me out." He added, "Robin, you do something I don't like. You're losing the bottom notes of the broken chords. You've got to catch them with the pedal. And those short, accented chords—not louder, drier. They need a nastiness about them."

In another, rhapsodic section, Robin said, "There's not enough color in this." Robin thinks Simon has such a wonderful sense of color when he plays—in general, he has always been known for this—that she has often wondered how he would paint. I asked how a pianist *got* color, and Simon said, pointing to his temple, "With the piano, what you hear in your head is what you get. You will never get any more out of an instrument than what you have in your ear and your imagination."

The concerto is a compelling work, and Robin asked, "Am I driving this section too much?"

He said, "I like the drive, but use less pedal."

Robin said, "It reminds me of Scott Fitzgerald—of the twenties. It's so poignant . . ."

Of a solo scherzando section, Simon said, "It's too timid, and not rhythmic enough. You're playing it too fast—it should sound carefree." She repeated the passage, which slows into two measures of sensuous chords that set up the entrance of the orchestra, and Simon said, "That was delicious."

As he played, he continued to squint at the music. He was too accustomed to the solo part. He said, "This is good training for you to play with a bad conductor. I'm getting you ready for life."

Of a grandiose passage with orchestra and piano together, Simon warned, "You're going to have to stretch that phrase. There isn't a conductor in the world who isn't going to stretch it, bask in it." She said, "And I'm waiting with my little triplets, wondering, How long, Oh Lord, how long?"

The slow movement, a leisurely andante, has solo trumpet threaded throughout, almost as important as the piano. The melody is jazzy at times, and the mood blues. Simon said, "Don't cover the trumpet. It's his big moment. Besides, he'll kill you." Robin complained, "Again, I'm dropping the bass notes of the rolled chords."

The final, allegro movement has brilliant toccata-like piano passages, rapid, repeated notes, a wild and bold orchestration, with xylophone and percussion and a constantly changing meter. Robin says there is so much going on in the orchestra, so much rhythmic complexity in the piece, that the pianist can easily lose his center of gravity.

Simon said, "You don't play concertos in small halls. Play it *out*. And there's a ring in that upper register. Let it *ring*." She backtracked, tried it, and said, "You're right."

He said, "You know I like inner voices, and you're losing out there. You're not bringing them out." She said, "I don't know. I'm afraid of losing the top line." She tried it again, and he said, "Delicious." She played a three-octave run in triplets, and he stopped. "Do it this way. A glissando instead of the triplets. It's smoother, has more brilliance, and conductors love it. A small *luftpause* and you're there, waiting for him to come in, and the connection with the orchestra is easy."

Simon went back to the opening of the third movement. "It should be more angular, more pointed in sound." There was a tutti section, and Robin said, "Do you play this business here?"

Simon said, "No. It's very hard to play. Conductors consider it their moment of glory, and they won't want you tagging along." It was followed by rapid repeated notes in the piano, and he said, "Keep them even. Your way leaves me unsatisfied, and I don't like anything that leaves me unsatisfied."

Robin laughed and said, "Well, we certainly can't have that."

Simon said, "Be a little sneakier about that rest." He played the passage and the difference was almost inaudible to me. Still, she said, "That's delightfully licentious."

Toward the end of a jazz section, he said, "Why so ladylike, so strict—a girl who can play jazz the way you do? Let *go!*"

Robin laughed again, and said, "I'm only programmed to turn on after five, and at twelve I self-destruct."

In the excitement of the climax to the last movement, Simon suddenly began playing the solo part. Robin said, "Out! That's *my* part." With a twinkle in her eye, she said to Chelle, "Once a soloist always a soloist."

Robin was flying all over the country that season, either for solo concerts or duo recitals with Ricci. She played the Rachmaninoff Second with the Great Falls Symphony, in

Great Falls, Montana, two nights in a row, and not only got standing ovations but was immediately reëngaged for the following year. After a duo recital with Ricci in Wichita, on March 30th, she returned to New York to find a letter from the Martha Baird Rockefeller Fund telling her that she had received a grant for an Alice Tully Hall recital—$3,500, the maximum grant for an individual artist, and the only one given to a pianist that year. Robin said, "I've *never* been so excited. I called everyone I knew, and no one was home. I sat down and polished my boots and tried to simmer down. And then I ran out and bought a bottle of champagne and went down to the Barrett offices." She laughed at herself. "Robin, the great provider. One bottle of champagne for twenty people."

Young recitalists like to play something not often played in New York—a premier of a piece is especially desirable, since it is bound to draw the critics, who will want to hear the new work and can't miss hearing the performer in the process. The same principle applies to a record. There's not much point in competing the first time around with Horowitz or Rubinstein if you can avoid it, and why record a sonata that already has fourteen listings in the Schwann catalogue? After consulting with Seymour Solomon at Vanguard Records, Robin planned to record a work rarely heard and never recorded—three movements of Stravinsky's *Firebird Suite,* as arranged for piano by Guido Agosti—a majestic, virtuosic masterpiece, whose pianistic technical demands defeat many performers. On the flip side, she would do Moussorgsky's *Pictures at an Exhibition.* The latter is a war-horse, but it is a piece Robin plays especially well. She was already thinking of October 29th, the date set for her Alice Tully Hall recital. She'd picked the program, which would be capped with the Stravinsky. She would open with her old love, the Ravel *Miroirs*—a daring move, considering the tremendous control, delicacy, finesse it requires—and then play a late Beethoven, the Opus 101. After intermission, she would do two Chopin études, each followed by an étude Leopold Godowsky had written as a study based on the Chopin. Robin said of the Godowskys, "They're extremely treacherous technically. Abbey gave them to me for my birthday, and he said, 'These are so tough you may never speak to me again.' They're difficult to figure out linearly, because Godowsky was such a subtle, imaginative man. And a fantastic pianist. He has all these little voices going at the same time. The pieces are like jigsaw puzzles. You have to figure out which notes you want to bring out and which you want to be subordinate. He had a theory that since the left hand is not used as much as the right, it's actually more flexible and capable of more finesse, and a number of the études are for left hand alone, and I'll do one of those." (Two days after Robin's recital, the girl in the polka-dot dress, still using the name Lily von Ballmoos, would give a Carnegie Recital Hall program; it was Halloween, and the hand-printed orange-and-black flyers announced that she would play nothing but Godowsky.) Robin said, "It's beautiful, elegant music. I'll also play Chopin's Polonaise-Fantaisie in A Flat, Opus 61, and finish with the Stravinsky—which may finish me."

In April, Dean Waldrop asked Robin if she would be the head of Juilliard's Secondary Piano Department. Robin was pleased. "He told me, 'I know that doesn't sound like it will coincide with the direction you want your life to take, but we'll give you a full-time assistant, and it won't interfere with your travel schedule. And it will give you financial security. And besides, we'd like to keep you around.' I was flattered. It was a vote of confidence, an indication of his estimation of me. Needless to say, I accepted."

Robin passed her doctoral oral exams in a record forty minutes. Her examiners asked few questions, and summed up the session by saying, "You know more about the subject than we do."

I was curious about how Robin felt in her new role—all the travel, racing for a plane, not knowing what kind of audience she'd have, what kind of piano. She said, "I'm sometimes a little nervous, but I never think 'I wish I didn't have to do this.' I like playing too much for that. But it's always a big deal—getting off that plane, wondering who will meet you and if they'll be easy to talk to. I like people, and I want them to like me. I try to draw them out. There's always someone in charge of you in a new town, and you hope it will be someone you can have a comfortable relationship with. But I do get nervous about what kind of piano I'll get. The office makes my hotel reservations. The girl who does it is very good. She'll say, 'We have el cheapo, middle of the road, and first class.' I usually ask for middle of the road. On planes I prefer reading to talking, and try to make that obvious to a seatmate. It's valuable time for me—time to relax, collect myself. I'm independent-minded, and I need solitude. I think that's one reason I'm drawn to music. There is solitude in music. There's just you and the music, and you are the protagonist."

She had just come back from a concert with the St. Louis Symphony, and she had quite a bit to say about that:

"There was a guest conductor, Eric Kunzel, and we were staying in the same hotel. At ten in the morning, we shared a cab to the rehearsal—the only one we would have—and to my horror I discovered from him that there'd been a mixup. I was scheduled to play the *Rhapsody in Blue*, which is currently not in my repertoire. I'd brought the Concerto in F. In desperation, I suggested twelve different concertos, but he said, 'It's an all-Gershwin program.' He added that if the orchestra had the parts for the concerto, we could do it—with an underrehearsed orchestra, I said to myself. As it turned out, the parts *were* available and the orchestra was top-notch." (In August, the pianist Alan Marks, who was scheduled to play the Gershwin concerto, would have to play the *Rhapsody* instead.)

"I often talk to myself in hotel rooms—to soothe myself, get rid of anxieties about the performance, give myself a pep talk. This time, I talked up a storm. 'You fool.' I was shaken out of my mind. Mad at the world. 'You idiot! Why do you do this? Why didn't you check with the office? *Double*check? You *know* there can be mixups. Idiot. You didn't play well at rehearsal. You let yourself be cowed by circumstances. You're not going to play well tonight. You don't look good, either. Your hair is a mess.' I'd ordered food from room service—I felt half starved—and the boy who brought the tray said, 'I only brought enough for one.' I was talking so much that he thought there were two people there." She paused for a moment, and then went on, "I usually do an about-face and start trying to cheer myself up. 'Well, you look pretty. They'll like you, and you haven't bombed yet. There's no reason you will tonight.' Actually, the concert went very well." In fact, Robin got another standing ovation, and was invited to come back the following year.

"That bluesy slow movement," Robin continued, "with the dialogue between piano and trumpet. The trumpet player was a girl, and she played the *dirtiest* blues I've ever heard. It was fantastic. We were grinning at each other. She was a marvel. In general, I've been lucky with orchestra concerts. You can tell in about five minutes how it's going to go. Walking out to rehearse, you'll see a smiling face, and you smile back. The conductors I've had have been marvelous accompanists. Sympathetic, great rapport. And the standards are so high these days that even semiprofessional orchestras are excellent. Some of the players are fantastic. The principal cellist in Great Falls was incredible. One would have to be a stone not to acknowledge the great solo she played in the Rachmaninoff."

Alan Weiss got his doctor's degree in June of 1977, and the same month he and Makiko were married. Makiko was working for her master's degree, and Alan was teaching, building his repertoire, and playing as many concerts as he could get. In October, he had a number of concerto concerts in Mexico, arranged by a conductor-friend of his, and got wonderful reviews: "Weiss conquered us with his enormous sensitivity and elegance of expression. . . ." "This esteemed artist has a great aesthetic message to transmit." In February, he had taped a recital, "The Art of Alan Weiss," in Michigan for educational television, to be shown throughout the country in the near future.

Still, he was discouraged. He was twenty-eight and concerned about his career, and he decided to enter one more competition, the Queen Elisabeth of Belgium. He had paid his own way to the Leeds Competition, in England, two years earlier, where he made it to the semifinals. This time he would go on a grant from the Institute of Professional Education, which is funded by the State Department. He was leaving the first of June, and I stopped by his apartment in the West Seventies to wish him well. Alan seemed less intense, had filled out a bit, no longer looked so boyish. The Weisses had an upright piano in the bedroom and a Steinway grand in the living room. Alan told me that he and Makiko took turns practicing on the Steinway, and he added, "When we're both practicing, we brace mattresses against each side of the door, so we won't hear each other." Makiko, a petite, pretty, spirited girl, is as serious about having a career as Alan is, and Alan considers her a phenomenal talent. Alan said that someday they might team up and do some two-piano concerts. Makiko, who is five years younger than Alan, had lived in New York since she was ten. I wondered if she had been brushed by women's lib, and kiddingly said, "Don't get to be *too* good." She laughed and said teasingly, "I'm already better than Alan."

Europe's heritage of classical music—children were raised on its richness—is reflected in Europeans' attitude about music. They are hungry for it, and many an American musician in earlier days started a career there by renting a hall, giving a concert, and getting a review. As one American pianist said, "In Europe, people don't come to hear the Beethoven 101. They come to hear how *you* play it." Classical record sales there are three to four times America's five percent of total record sales.

The Queen Elisabeth is perhaps the jewel of all competitions. The money prizes are high, the repertoire requirements mammoth, the competition fierce. Placing first is a guarantee of success. In New York, many Leventritt contestants had trouble finding a place to stay, and were desperate for a piano to practice on. In Brussels, eighty-two pianists were put up in private homes and given excellent pianos to practice on. Two months before the competition, each contestant had been sent a work, commissioned from a Belgian composer, to be played during the preliminaries, which were perhaps harder on the judges than the pianists. The judges, sitting in the first row so they could see the pianists' hands, heard each contestant play the Haydn Variations in F Minor—a work that can be deadly monotonous unless the tempo is just right and it is played with great imagination, revealing the personal taste of the performer. But, as Robin had said, when everyone plays the same piece, it can be very telling.

The preliminaries and the semifinals were held in an auditorium in the Conservatoire de Musique, which held eight hundred people and was filled throughout the event. Furthermore, to accommodate those who could not get in, the preliminaries and the semifinals were broadcast on the radio and the finals were televised. Also, the public was encouraged, as the contest progressed, to send in postcards naming their favorites. All eighty-two received at least one review in one of four Brussels newspapers, and finalists were reviewed four times. Twenty-three contenders made it to the semifinals, and Alan was one of them. And when the twenty-three were pared to ten, he was still in the running. The ten were housed in the Chapelle Musical, an estate outside Brussels, where they spent a week learning another commissioned work, a *concerto imposé*. They were not permitted to make phone calls or go into town unescorted—a guarantee that no one could get advice from a teacher. An American observer said that during the semifinals Douglas Finch, a Canadian pianist, and Brigitte Ingerer, a French pianist, were the favorites of the audience. They were called back for repeated bows and were besieged by autograph seekers after it was all over.

In the week of the finals, the World Soccer Cup playoffs were televised in Belgium, and the competition and the playoffs drew an equal number of viewers. The competition finals, like the soccer playoffs, had commentators discussing and explaining to the viewers what they were seeing and hearing. During that round Alan was the standout —the audience's favorite. Still, the judges ranked him fourth (Douglas Finch was fifth), and Alan was disappointed, because he was pleased with the way he'd played and felt he should have placed higher—perhaps second. So did Liliane Weinstadt, a concert manager in Brussels, who sought out Alan backstage and asked to represent him in Europe. And so did the critic of *Le Soir*, Brussels' equivalent of the *New York Times*, who headed his review "The Poet," and went on to say:

> The poet is this young American, Alan Weiss, who during these weeks has so intrigued us with the manner he possesses of engaging in a very personal dialogue with his music, a rapport whose meaning sometimes eluded us.
>
> All reticence fell this evening. It no longer occurred to me to speak of the tediousness of repeated hearings of the *concerto imposé*; Alan Weiss transfigured all this. By some kind of magic, radiance emanating from his performance, he is capable of transforming worthless lead into the purest gold.
>
> With extraordinary phrasing of expressive exactness in Chopin's Fourth Scherzo; with varied colors express-

ing the radiance and the violence of the soul; with a subtlety unaffected but merging into infinite perspectives, the extreme variety of sound he obtained from the piano revealed his creative imagination. Each note was the expression of a deep involvement with the work.

One has rarely heard the Brahms D Minor Piano Concerto interpreted with such authority and eloquence. The grand sweep of each movement was drawn with great inspiration and a nobility that did not hinder the dramatic side from forcefully asserting itself; with subtle transitions, the great cadences were admirably integrated into the sumptuous discourse of the first movement, where Brahms seems to want to break away in pathetic and stormy combat from the somber realities of the human condition; Alan Weiss's sensitivity and imagination, at all times, avoided the pomp that threatens this music.

How he draws with infinite tenderness an abandon without affectation the great sweep of the Adagio's reverie, to at last escape into a sort of freedom finally conquered with decision and vitality in the Rondo Finale. And once again, this palette of varied and radiant sounds, this way of making silence speak, this magic of an art that always passes through the heart before bursting through the fingers . . .

Alan signed a contract with Miss Weinstadt before he left Brussels. If he hadn't placed higher in the competition, still it had served as an important showcase for him. His tenacity had finally paid off, and he was on his way.

Chapter
II

Before Robin left for the summer for Puyallup and then Shawnigan, she spent two days recording the Moussorgsky and the Stravinsky. She was touched by the concern shown by Mme. Dorfmann, who had called Robin every few hours over the weekend to give her pep talks. She urged her to get all dressed up, to "look pretty. I always did." Robin, partly for financial reasons, had not officially studied with anyone for almost two years; she had already satisfied Juilliard's piano requirements for a doctor's degree. But Mme.

Dorfmann took a special interest in her, and frequently, when she had a free hour, would give her a lesson; Robin sought her help with certain recital pieces, and Mme. Dorfmann was generous with her time.

Robin recorded the *Pictures at an Exhibition* on Monday, and reported to me that she was somewhat stunned by Seymour Solomon's musical acumen. She had felt good about her *Pictures*—most people think she has a special affinity for the work, and like her interpretation—but Solomon stopped her after the first "Promenade." "He told me it was much too fast; I couldn't imagine playing it slower, and I argued with him." Moussorgsky composed *Pictures* to commemorate an artist-friend of his, Victor Alexandrovich Hartmann, who died tragically at the age of thirty-nine. At a memorial exhibition of his works, strolling back and forth and studying various paintings, Moussorgsky was inspired to honor his friend, and he composed *Pictures*.

"Mr. Solomon told me that Moussorgsky was a *big* man, and walking through an art exhibit, 'promenading,' he would *not* move briskly. He was right, though it was hard for me to give in. My brain was almost grooved for my tempo. In the end, I did it his way."

Robin recorded the Stravinsky on Tuesday, and I went along to listen, and get acquainted with the piece (I had never heard the piano version before). Robin had called it "a mammothly difficult work," and she added, "Maybe one should be a member of the Flying Wallendas to play the piece—it requires extreme deterity, agility, and an almost athletic prowess at the piano to maintain the scope and pacing while meeting the technical demands of the work." She described to me the three movements of the piece. "The first movement, the 'Infernal Dance,' is the most taxing physically, with its syncopations, jagged rhythms, and quick changes of mood. The performer must try to convey all the colors of the orchestra. In the slow movement, the 'Berceuse,' the nuance of the melody line, laconic and hypnotic, is very difficult to sustain on the piano. Also, one must try to reproduce the effect of pizzicato strings and dark orchestral harmonic colors that surround this hypnotic line. The 'Finale' begins with a folkish Slavic melody in the 'horns,' and the piano maintains a pianissimo tremolo under this line, which gradually must unfold as the firebird unfurls its plumage. It's hard to gauge. There's a temptation to overdo the long crescendo as the volume mounts. Finally, the movement explodes into a full orchestra-like section of repeated glissandi from the bottom to the top of the keyboard while the firebird's theme blasts forth with massive chords. If you give too much too soon, it's instant death."

The recording setup was an odd one. Solomon, to get the best acoustical arrangement possible, had rented a Masonic temple, a building abutting the Vanguard studios to the south. A cable was wound around the corner from the control room half a city block into the temple's auditorium —a vast amphitheatre, seating two thousand, with high, vaulted ceilings adorned with rococo bas-relief figures, which were blue and flecked with gold. Needless to say, Robin and the producers—Seymour Solomon and Joanna Nickrenz, an editor-producer at Elite Records, who had been hired to edit the record—could not see one another. (Abbey Simon was pleased for Robin that Ms. Nickrenz would edit the tape. He thinks she's the best in the business, and calls her "the lady with the golden scissors.") Solomon's instructions to Robin were a disembodied voice coming through a microphone. On the floor beside her, Robin had a can of baby powder, which she frequently sprinkled on her fingers. It was hot in the room, and the keys of the piano—one she liked and that Solomon had gone to great lengths to get for her—were plastic, and sometimes needed dusting, too. The piano also needed frequent tuning because of the workout it got with the Stravinsky, and a tuner was there for that purpose. The piece in some sections sounds like four pianos going at once, and to achieve this effect the pianist is exerting tremendous strength on a delicate instrument. Robin said to Solomon, "I expected to lose my lease while I learned this." The score of the work was on the floor beside her for consultation purposes. She can't stand performing with music. She feels the printed work gets between her and the instrument. She'd been more nervous about the recording session than any concert—she kept thinking of it as being for posterity. Even though her playing elicited an occasional "Bravo!" from Solomon, she was, as usual, her own worst critic, and often insisted on doing one more take, though Solomon had considered the last one excellent.

After Take 93, Solomon said, "That wraps it up, I think."

Robin came into the control room and said, "I'd like to do it over."

Solomon asked, "The last take?" and Robin said, "No. The whole thing. I'm not happy with the way I played."

Solomon looked incredulous, and told her, "You'll kill yourself." Robin tried to persist, but Solomon was firm.

Robin and I left the studio together, and on our way out she said, "If nothing else, that was the best practicing I've ever done." She was still bothered with the way certain passages had gone, but she would not know until the fall,

when she would hear the lacquer, if her fears were un-
founded.

Robin came back to New York in time to supervise entrance exams in her department at Juilliard on September
12th. And then she settled in to really master her Tully
Hall program. (The report from Solomon on the recording
was good; now she had to have color photographs taken for
the record jacket. Some companies hang on to a record for
as long as two years before releasing it. Robin was pleased
that Vanguard planned to release hers as soon as possible.)
New York was into its second month of a newspaper strike,
and all over town musicians were cursing a fate that led
them to get all revved up for concerts for which there
would be virtually no reviews. While the New York *Post*
had just returned to publication, and was churning along,
trying to satisfy all readers' needs (and generally short-
changing everyone), it had never mattered that much to
musicians; the paper skipped at least half the concerts in
town. It was the *Times* that counted, and it appeared there
would be no *Times* published after Robin's recital.

Barrett had always taken a special interest in Robin, and
he lined up three out-of-town concerts for her, at which she
could play her recital program, to get ready for the big
event. He suggested that she rearrange the order of the
program—do the Chopin or the Stravinsky in the first half
instead of the Beethoven. He reminded her, in case the
strike ended, that critics sometimes don't stay for an entire
program, and Robin was emerging as strong in Romantic,
Impressionist, and pyrotechnical works. Actually, Barrett
was slightly apprehensive about the Beethoven. Most
young pianists avoid the late Beethoven sonatas; there's a

very good chance that they won't please the critics, who often don't agree among themselves about how they should be played or which concert artist does the best by them. Most of Beethoven's late works, written when the composer could no longer hear, have a profound, unearthly quality that is hard to capture—"ambiguous and yearning" in the Opus 101, according to Robin. It concludes with one of his complex fugues that stretch the performer's technical abilities to the limit. Barrett possibly wished she would avoid a late Beethoven altogether for such a crucial concert. But Robin likes the way she plays the piece, feels her interpretation is valid and convincing, and, proving again that she's a pianist who takes chances, was adamant. She thought the impact of the Beethoven would be lessened if it was followed immediately by the Stravinsky, and, in her mind, there was a nice thread, an order, in her arrangement of the pieces. She felt the Beethoven, with its linear clarity, would contrast beautifully with the dense texture and rich palette of the Ravel. And she didn't consider either one what she calls "stand up and cheer" music. The Chopin études—early works, "salon music" in his day—would be easy for the audience to get into after the intermission. The Chopin Polonaise-Fantaisie, one of his last works, more majestic than the études, and building to a climax with a sequence of musical statements, would prepare the audience for the Stravinsky.

Robin did the program in Mexico, Missouri; Duluth, Minnesota; and Fort Worth, Texas. In Mexico, Missouri, her heart sank at the sight of a five-and-a-half-foot piano— a miniature grand. (The local auspices wanted to rent a concert grand in St. Louis, but the cost was prohibitive.) She tried it for a few minutes, and then went back to her hotel room and watched the World Series. How could she possibly play the Stravinsky on that Tinker Toy?

Robin is good at talking to audiences, explaining what she's about to do. She might have been the first pianist in Mexico (population 15,000) with a serious program, and she gave a short talk before each piece, being especially detailed with the *Miroirs,* since the names of each movement were in French.

Robin's parents came to New York for the recital, and Mrs. McCabe helped Robin choose a dress—a pale-peach chiffon. Robin got the Steinway of her choice "with some manipulation"—it was one of the company's best, and it was "piano week" in the city. Three pianists—including Alicia de Larrocha—were playing in various halls in the city on the same day as Robin. She was able to practice on the piano a number of times—get to know it, what she could get from it, what responses to expect. On the day of the recital, between a church service held in Tully Hall and the Lincoln Center Chamber Music Society's five-o'clock concert, Robin took her parents down to the hall and invited them onstage so they could see how an auditorium looked from her point of view. Back in her apartment, she was drawn to her own piano every few minutes, just to fiddle around. Pop, jazz, anything, just to be in touch with it. Robin told me Chelle was with her, and was good support when Robin let off steam: "What a silly damn business. I must be crazy to let myself in for this. Ridiculous!" Robin said, "Chelle always knows the right thing to say, and it's usually so full of common sense. Anyone else would get on my nerves. She came down to the hall with me and talked for a while. Actually, I like to be alone, which she knows, and she didn't stay long. And Mr. Barrett came back to wish me luck. The week before, Nathaniel Rosen, the cellist—he won the Tchaikovsky *and* the Naumburg—played in Tully Hall, and the stagehand had wandered off to get a drink of water. When Nat had finished his first number and tried to leave the stage, those great, massive, slatted doors were firmly shut. I pleaded with the stagehand to *be* there after the Ravel. I told him that I was coming offstage then, and I didn't want to have to scratch on the door."

Robin likes Tully Hall because it has a deep backstage. She's taking a course in body movement, so she'll be as comfortable getting to the piano as she is while she's playing it. That short walk is a problem with many performers; often their torsos precede their legs by seconds, and the temptation to look down, instead of head *up,* is strong. Maybe someone's foot is sticking out, if the concert is with orchestra, or a beam has been left by a carpenter. To start from the edge of the stage, one can look tentative; Robin told the stagehand she was going to start as far back as possible, so she would be in full stride when she appeared before the audience.

The hall—partly because of the newspaper strike (an ad in the *Times,* offering reduced prices for senior citizens and students, can help fill a hall)—was not full, but those who were there had come because they truly wanted to: an ideal audience. In addition to relatives and friends, there were many pianists present—Juilliard students, a number of faculty members, and other pianist friends of Robin's.

When she appeared, she looked radiant and purposeful, and a few minutes into the Ravel it was clear that she was enjoying herself. It takes the daring of a cat burglar to begin a program with that piece, but she was in total control. She put her own stamp on the Beethoven, playing it with assurance and conviction. The second half of the concert was stunning: she displayed a virtuoso technique and an obvious love of the instrument and the pieces she was playing. Toward the end of the Chopin E-Flat Minor Étude for Left Hand Alone, she braced her right hand under the fingerboard to keep tension in the hand—ready for the treacherous "Black Key" Étude, which came next. The E-Flat Minor Étude was performed with such beauty and elegance that the audience broke into applause, and there were shouts of "Bravo!" The Polonaise was truly majestic, and the *Firebird* electrifying. When she finished, there was a slight pause before the audience burst into applause. Two ushers presented her with four bouquets, and after several bows, she placed the flowers on the floor, in front of the piano, and for an encore played the Abram Chasins transcription of the "Dance of the Blessed Spirits," flute music from Gluck's *Orpheus*—an elegiac, haunting, yet serenely beautiful ending to the evening.

At the reception that followed, Robin was relaxed and happy, pleased with her performance.

Two days later, the *Post* printed a review, by Harriett Johnson, that shattered Robin, hurt her parents, and baffled her friends—especially those who were pianists themselves. Miss Johnson opened the review with a jab at Robin's appearance, saying that Robin had looked gauche in an orange dress that accentuated bad posture. Several *more* things for young pianists to worry about. Miss Johnson seemed surprised that the Ravel was good, and she said, "Miss McCabe proved that she is primarily a colorist who excels in dramatizing miniatures and she was very successful in the opening Ravel *Miroirs*. Her 'Une Barque sur l'Ocean' flashed with shimmering arabesques and cascading runs. She evoked distant bells in 'La Vallée des Cloches' and altogether stirred the imagination. She dramatized the varied 'reflections' in a most musical manner, giving them perspective and nuance."

She didn't like the Beethoven, said it was "far less meaningful in interpretation. The 'Adagio ma non troppo, con affetto,' however, surprisingly, was deeply felt and so communicated." She went on to say that Robin "glossed over" the "Allegretto ma non troppo" and called her "technically inadequate" for the "Allegro." She listed but did not review the Chopin-Godowsky and the Polonaise-Fantaisie. In an about-face, Miss Johnson praised the Stravinsky-Agosti, saying Robin "raised quite a stir, getting over the keys brilliantly and altogether outdoing herself dramatically. In truth, interpretatively, she became a veritable firebird herself."

For several days, Robin was destroyed by the review, and her parents stayed on to "help pick up the pieces." Abbey Simon assured Robin that, with the exception of the vicious first paragraph, it was a review a young pianist might be pleased with. Simon, like many established artists, tends to view the press with a jaundiced eye. Newspaper criticism seems most of the time an exercise in futility; what Miss Brogan had told Robin about a jury's tendency to make negative comments when asked to write reactions might just as easily apply to music critics. (Two weeks later, playing the same program at UCLA, Robin received a standing ovation, and the critic for the Los Angeles *Times* said, in part: "Her technique is formidable for accuracy, strength, speed and finger independence. Her command of styles reaches far. She played two études of Chopin and their matching transcriptions by Leopold Godowsky as charmingly and with as much easy authority and stylistic bite as one might wish. And she brought down the house with a reading of the Polonaise-Fantaisie at once poetic, heroic, spontaneous and tightly wound.")

Robin is resilient—she'll have to be for the career she has chosen—and she "picked up the pieces" and was off to the University of Wisconsin on November 6th for a four-day "residency"—a fairly new term in the music lexicon, and part of a trend to expand interest and understanding of music in America. As she explained it, "You go into a town for several days. In addition to giving a concert, you might hold a master class, or be interviewed on a local television show, or give additional concerts in schools, or talk to some young musicians in the community about their futures, or have lunch with the Symphony League. I gave several school concerts in Madison. In one school, to my surprise, the classes were kindergarten through third grade. Can you imagine? All those little urchins sitting on the floor and screaming. I couldn't possibly play anything in my standard repertoire. I don't read children very well. I did a quick mental double-take and said, 'I'm going to play a short piece about an animal. I'll give you one clue. It's an animal that flies. You listen, and see if you can guess what it is.' I played 'The Flight of the Bumblebee,' by Rimski-Korsakov. After I finished, there was no applause at all. I looked out at the audience and saw four hundred hands in the air. Without being called on, they started shouting, 'A rabbit!' 'A giraffe!' 'A hummingbird!' They were enthusiastic, and I was pleased that they had all been listening. I announced that the next piece would be about another animal, and I played 'The Ballet of the Chicks,' from *Pictures at an Exhibition,* and somebody got it. Once you get them listening, you can give them other things, deeper things. Next I said I would play a piece by Chopin—the 'Black Key' Étude—and in the right hand I would be playing only on the black keys. I told them to watch my right hand, and if they saw me strike a white key, they would know I'd made a mistake. After I'd finished, one little boy shouted, 'You made a mistake! I saw you hit a white key!'" She laughed at the memory, and said, "Actually, I didn't, but I sure had their attention. I played the theme from *Star Wars,* and said I would play requests, which was dangerous. There was a chorus of voices asking for *Grease.* I'd never seen it and I didn't know it. These kids are programmed on a different monitor than you or I. It startled me. You just have to do what you can. There were three or four school concerts, and I had no idea I was expected to do them. I lost track of how many times I played 'The Sting,' and it will be some time before I'll want to play another Scott Joplin rag. I threw in some serious things along the way. The principal told me that before me, that year, they'd seen a mime group and heard a guitar player —*not* classical. I ended up enjoying it. The nice thing is, you've given these children a good experience. In seven to ten years, a big-name pianist will come to town, and chances are some of them will want to go, because of that good experience. They'll remember that thing that happened to them when they were very young and that turned out to be not bad at all. In essence, I feel I turned some of them on to music. It would have been very easy to turn them off."

I saw Alan Weiss once more. In the fall, he had won a Phillips' Collection Competition in Washington, D.C., and had played two concerts there. Alan had once said to Firkusny that he could not play the way Firkusny did, but he would "strive to." Firkusny now calls Alan "one of the most brilliant pianists of his generation," and on the night of Robin's recital, October 29th, Alan and Firkusny did a Mozart concerto for two pianos with the Rochester Philharmonic, in Rochester, New York. And Firkusny asked Alan to record the entire Mozart literature for four hands and two pianos with him for Vox. It might be some time before they can do this, Alan told me, considering their schedules. Alan and Makiko were packing. In a week or so they would move to Brussels, where they would live. Alan's manager, Liliane Weinstadt, had booked quite a few concerts for him throughout Europe, and they might be gone for as long as seven months. They were excited about going, obviously looking forward to it.

I talked to Herbert Barrett again in the spring of 1979 to get his assessment of how Robin was doing, what the future might hold. I was being premature, since he had said during our first interview that it took at least three years to tell how well a newcomer like Robin would do in that crowded field. But he beamed while he talked to me: "The returns on Robin have been amazing—truly amazing. I told you that being a 'repeater' was essential in this business—being asked back. Well, she certainly is a repeater. And her growth in every respect in the past year has been dramatic, too. She had twenty concerts—fantastic for the first year. And the mail we get about her is wonderful. She's twice the pianist she was when I signed her, and she keeps growing.

And she has great courage. I myself never dreamt it would happen this fast. I see a very big future for her."

The 1976 Leventritt Competition was probably the last. The foundation feels that it can help young musicians in a more direct, less painful way. Many promising performers are known in the music world from their teachers' opinions and their track records in schools, and they are being auditioned by judges chosen by the foundation in fairly serene circumstances. Also, the 1976 finalists have been given more attention in terms of management and concerts than previous finalists. Robin told me about the Leventritt in the late spring. And she brought me up to date: Richard Fields had become the accompanist of Lotte Goslar's Pantomime Circus—a successful group that toured throughout Europe. Richard was pleased that the music included some of the best works in the standard piano repertoire, and in a number of cities in Europe the critics singled him out and praised his playing. His repertoire was increasing, and he was renewing ties he'd made in the Boston area when he was still in high school. In the summer, he would play concertos with a number of semi-professional symphonies in New England. If he'd ever seriously considered entering a competition, he no longer cared. He said that no one even remembered the name of the pianist who won first in the last Tchaikovsky in Moscow. There were so many competitions they were beginning to negate each other. He planned to get his doctor's degree, though he hadn't decided where. His memories of Juilliard are fond, but he wants the experience of going to a different school. Bloch had almost circled the globe, playing concerts, in the past year, and had gone to Chile to judge a big competition. He'd been at Shawnigan the previous summer (Robin has a funny snapshot, taken by Chelle standing on the piano, of herself with Simon and Bloch playing a piece for six hands; what a tangle), and he planned to return, as did Simon. Roman was still doing some accompanying at Juilliard, and several times I saw him turning pages for other pianists at Tully Hall chamber-music concerts. Chelle had some concerts lined up in the Northwest, and she and Robin would both go to Shawnigan, but this time Chelle would be a faculty assistant, instead of a student. Also, she had accepted a teaching fellowship at the University of Michigan, beginning in the fall, and would not be returning to Juilliard.

I asked Robin whether—now that she had her final degree—she still wanted to live in the Northwest and teach, and have Barrett book concerts for her from there. She thought for a minute, and then she said, "This past year has made me realize that my center of gravity is here. This is where I belong, where I ought to be. To put it more accurately, this is where I *want* to be."